From Freud to Frankl

Our Modern Search for Personal Meaning

John H. Morgan

Wyndham Hall Press

FROM FREUD TO FRANKL

Our Modern Search for Personal Meaning

John H. Morgan
B.A., M.A., Ph.D., D.Sc.

Library of Congress Catalog Card Number
86-050580

ISBN 0-932269-92-3

"Tell man that he is an end in himself,
and his answer will be despair."

--Rabbi Abraham Joshua Heschel

For Linda, Kendra, Bethany, and Kyna,
Who fill my life with love, joy, and peace.

... In Appreciation ...

To Yale University, for appointment as a
"Postdoctoral Research Fellow,"

To the University of Chicago, for appointment as a
"Postdoctoral Scholar,"

To Princeton Theological Seminary, for appointment as a
"Visiting Fellow,"

To The University of Notre Dame, for appointments as a
"National Science Foundation Science Faculty Fellow"

and "Postdoctoral Research Associate in the
History and Philosophy of Science."

TABLE OF CONTENTS

INTRODUCTION

The challenge of ancient man was "how to die" in a world which reflected the heavenly abode to which he was destined. The challenge of modern man is "how to live" in a world seemingly devoid of meaning and purpose. Modern man's readiness to despair, his inclination to cynicism, and his sadistic enjoyment of self-flagellation all bespeak the current crisis of meaning. Whether one turns to the press, the television and Hollywood, or the publishing house, there is the portrayal of the search for and absence of a sense of direction and meaning in the life of the individual and in that of society at large. From Auschwitz to Vietnam, from "Easy Rider" to the "Last Tango in Paris," from Adolf Hitler to Charles Manson, the depravity of man is so blatantly clear, we are inevitably thrown into an inquiry as to the meaning of life. Is there or is there not "meaning" to life? Is meaninglessness or meaning the answer? Is man nothing more than "a two-legged animal without feathers" or is he a "collaborator with God"?

In the following pages, we shall explore the breadth of options in answering the modern question of life's meaning. Though most of the literature of the 20th century has in one manner or another struggled with the question of meaning in human experience, and therefore, to select this writer or book to that one borders on the arbitrary; nevertheless, I have chosen those who are at least exemplary of the major addresses to the question. In addition to being selective as to the writers discussed in this study, I have been equally selective in that piece of literature from each writer to which I wish to address the question of meaning. If the reader wishes to develop a comprehensive understanding of the thought of Freud or Sartre or Teilhard de Chardin or any of the other thinkers being considered here, this little study is hardly the place to end, though it certainly constitutes a reasonable beginning.

Bristol, Indiana   JHM
1988

CHAPTER ONE

"From Pleasure to Reality"

"...what decides the purpose of life is simply
the programme of the pleasure principle."

--Sigmund Freud (1856-1939)

Introduction

Sigmund Freud's classic, CIVILIZATION AND ITS DISCONTENTS,
will be reviewed for its address to and perspective on the meaning
of human life, especially as conceived in the context of human development which inevitably counter-poses the principle of **pleasure**
with the principle of **reality**. In this chapter, we will hear Freud
say "...the purpose of life is simply the programme of the pleasure
principle," and since man is unable (for personal reasons) or not
permitted (for social reasons) to gratify his desire for pleasure,
he must learn that "satisfaction is obtained from illusions..." The
tensions resulting from the desire for pleasurable gratification on
the one hand and the encounter with social reality on the other hand
make for a life-experience characterized by anxiety and neurosis
which are most readily coped with through illusions. Therefore,
in a real sense, says Freud, "...our civilization is largely responsible
for our misery..." What then can the meaning of life be? is a question
Freud pursues.*

§ § §

The impact that Freud's thought has had upon Western culture in
the last 75 years is profound. Since the publishing of his DIE TRAUM-

---

*Unless otherwise noted, all quotations are from Freud's CIVILIZA-
TION AND ITS DISCONTENTS (1930).

DENTUNG, 1900 (THE INTERPRETATION OF DREAMS, 1955), Freud's thought has gained such widespread usage that it would be difficult to imagine a modern world devoid of his contributions to the understanding of the individual in society. If his studies of the human psyche have revolutionized man's thoughts about and attitudes toward the unconscious, his writings on religion, society, and culture have shaken older images of human experiences and ushered in a new era of religious and social theorizing.

Not unaware of the profound shock his thought would have cn modern man, Freud saw himself in a select line of great minds who have shaken the Western World. There have been three narcissistic shocks to Western man, thought Freud. First was the Copernican or Cosmilogical shock which shook Western man loose from his anthropogeocentric cosmology which located man and the earth at the center of the universe. This rude awakening brought trauma to Western men who then had to learn how to live in a world where neither man nor the earth could claim centrality, but rather had been pre-empted by a heleocentric cosmology. The sun, a gaseous ball devoid of life, became the center.

The second and equally traumatic shock to Western man was dealt by Charles Darwin -- the Biological Shock -- which demonstrated the biological relatedness of all living things, man included. If Copernicus had challenged the status of man in the universe, Darwin had surely succeeded in establishing the dependence of man upon the earth and his kinship with all earth's creatures. The fact that man had persisted even after Copernicus in an anthropocentrism which over-valued the differences between man and animals as well as between various genetic groupings within the human family made even more difficult the acceptance of Darwin's revelation. To this very day, there are vocal if not large pockets of supposedly modern men who still decry the atheism erroneously assumed implicit in Darwin's biology and still lay claim to a primitive worldview nurtured by a creation-story literalism.

Last and most profound of the shocks to Western man has been the Psychological Shock mercilessly dealt by Sigmund Freud. The shock was ushered in by a succession of scientific bomb-blasts: THE INTERPRETATION OF DREAMS (1911), TOTEM AND TABOO (1912), BEYOND THE PLEASURE PRINCIPLE (1920), THE FUTURE OF AN ILLUSION (1927), and CIVILIZATION AND ITS DISCONTENTS (1930). By no means the whole bibliography of profound, challenging, and highly controversial studies, these works are exemplary of the breadth of Freud's research and interests. His study of the origin and function of religion, published under the significantly descriptive title, THE FUTURE OF AN ILLUSION, is without question his most controversial and most widely read study outside the specific field of psychoanalysis. And yet, his CIVILIZATION AND ITS DISCONTENTS, which reviews the arguments in the religion book, represents his most mature thoughts on human society and the individual's relation to it. David Bakan, in his provocative and highly controversial study on Freud, entitled, SIGMUND FREUD AND THE JEWISH MYSTICAL TRADITION (1969), has cogently argued that Freud was himself a most exemplary thinker in the Kabbalistic tradition of Jewish mysticism. Kabbalism was an esoteric tradition which chose for reasons of safety and privacy to speak of the human spiritual condition in terms of the dark mysteries and primitive symbolisms of sexuality. If Bakan is right in this bit of theorizing, then the following statement from Freud gains even more profound eminence in modern religious thought: "The tendency on the part of civilization to restrict sexual life is no less clear than its other tendency to expand the cultural unit." But let us look more closely at his work before we pass judgment on Freud's either apt or warped view of the human condition.

The opening remarks in this brief statement of Freud's under scrutiny here are in reference to a friend who, though he entirely agreed with Freud's analysis of religion in his 1927 study, was concerned to call himself religious on the basis of a "sensation of eternity" or "oceanic feeling." Not only was Freud disinclined to accept his friend's suggestion, but Freud also wished to demonstrate how his feeling of eternity corroborated the ego-development schema of psychoanalysis.

The emergence of the ego ("...there is nothing of which we are more certain than the feeling of ourself, of our own ego (p.12),") says Freud, is "through a process of development...(p.13)." The ego is developmentally the inevitable result of a confronting of the pristine libidinal impulses of the undifferentiated id with the external world of sheer actuality. The id, having its motivational impetus centered in the **pleasure-principle**, confronts the **reality-principle** as the individual infant begins to discover the unpleasantness of the otherness, separateness, and outsideness of the real world. There is a strong motivation on the part of the id-driven child to "separate from the ego everything that can become a source of such unpleasure, to throw it outside and to create a pure pleasure-ego which is confronted by a strange and threatening 'outside' (p.14)." The id begins necessarily to develop a negotiating capability -- the ego as executor of libidinal powers -- whereby the desires of the id are pacified with substitute gratifications which are physically accessible and socially acceptable. "In this way," says Freud, "one makes the first step towards the introduction of the reality principle which is to dominate future development (p.14)."

Freud is here explaining a scenario of ego-development which will address the issue of the oceanic feeling, and thus the subject of religion. This executive function of the differentiated ego serves as the primary medium of negotiation between the pleasurable desires from within (the raw libido of the id) and the realities of the outside world (social restraints upon behavior). The more responsible the ego is to the reality-principle, the greater the experience of separateness from the external world -- "Our present ego-feeling is, therefore, only a shrunken residue of a much more inclusive, indeed, an all-embracing feeling, which corresponded to a more intimate bond between the ego and the world about it (p. 15)." There, Freud concludes that to the extent that this earlier primary ego feeling of virtual undifferentiation of self and world in infancy has persisted alongside the narrower demarcated ego feeling of self separate from the world in maturity, there is the likelihood that feelings of "limitlessness and of a bond with the universe," i.e., the oceanic feeling, will be present.

Freud contends that "...in mental life nothing which has once been formed can perish...(p. 16)," and, therefore, such feelings as these considered here are simply the residue of infantile experience. And though Freud is reluctant to connect the feeling of "oneness with the universe" with the origins of religion, he is "perfectly willing to acknowledge that the 'oceanic' feeling exists in many people, and (is) inclined to trace it back to an early phase of ego-feeling." In conclusion to this topic of oceanic feelings, Freud is wont to trace the origins of the oceanic feeling to "a first attempt at a religious consolation," which is to say, a feeling resulting from the developing ego's growing awareness of the external world. Furthermore, he is anxious to rearticulate his 1927 theory of religious origins, which says that "The derivation of religious needs from the infant's helplessness and the longing for the father aroused by it...(is) incontrovertible, especially since the feeling is not simply prolonged from childhood days, but is permanently sustained by fear of the superior power of Fate (p. 16)." Though this point will be considered in a later context, it must be noted here that for Freud, the energy output demonstrated by the ego's undying efforts to responsibly direct the otherwise unbridled powers of the id is the result of a deep feeling whose function is the "expression of a strong need." The religious feeling, says Freud, is a source of energy because it is expressive of a powerful need, viz., the helpless infant's longing for a powerful father.

In considering religion, Freud consistently was "concerned much less with the deepest sources of the religious feeling than with what the common man understands by his religion...(p.2)." And yet, he was often so convincing in his critique of religion's object being nothing more than an "enormously exalted father" that it is difficult if not impossible to separate the "deepest" from the "common" in religion. Freud had no patience with the "great majority of mortals" who were infantilely dependent on this projected father-image as a substitute for ego-development and personal maturity. "The whole thing is so patently infantile," complained Freud, a painful reality that most men, avoiding true maturity, opt for a "pitiful rearguard" attachment to childish fantasies of a loving Providence which, watching over us, will reward us eternally in heaven if we are good.

The question of "the purpose of human life," says Freud, bespeaks man's "presumptuousness." Religion alone can answer this question, for the whole "idea of life having a purpose stands and falls with the religious system (p. 23)." And though these metaphysical complexities lie outside Freud's investigation here, he chooses to get at the question by an inquiry into the nature of human behavior which demonstrates man's purpose and intention in life. And in answer to this question, "What do men show by their behavior to be the purpose and intention of life?", Freud answers simply, "They strive after happiness, they want to become happy and to remain so." That is, they seek the "absence of pain and unpleasure" while seeking the "experiencing of strong feelings of pleasure." Therefore, Freud concludes, the rhetoric of religion to the contrary notwithstanding, "what decides the purpose of life is simply the programme of the pleasure principle."

Happiness, i.e, the satisfaction of needs too seldom gratified, is difficult to realize and impossible to sustain. Society is ever ready to condemn violations of its laws, and unrestrained self-gratification, i.e., personal happiness, inevitably results in a clash of the individual's desires (pleasure principle) and society's rules (reality principle). Therefore, "unhappiness is much less difficult to experience" because the individual is threatened with suffering from three sides: from our own body due to its finitude, from the external world with all its rules, and from our relations with other men. Since happiness is hardly possible at all, and never for any significant duration, man has necessarily had to develop techniques for controlling the instincts which given free rein would inevitably bring catastrophe to the individual and to society.

Through the executive services of the ego, the libidinal forces are displaced (focused upon a secondary and socially acceptable object choice) and the instincts are systematically sublimated. In the movement from pleasure to reality, the individual adopts two kinds of "satisfaction...obtained from illusion...(which arise out of) the imagination (p. 27)." Both religion and the enjoyment of the arts are the result of sublimated instincts and displaced libido. Freud says:

> A special importance attaches to the case in which this attempt to procure a certainty in happiness and a protection against suffering through a delusional remoulding of reality is made by a considerable number of people in common. The religions of mankind must be classed among the mass-delusions of this kind. No one, needless to say, who shares a delusion ever recognized it as such. (p. 28).

And, says Freud, those who define happiness in life as the pursuit and love of beauty fail to realizxe that aesthetic impulse is simply the result of an ungratified primary sexual motivation. The tensions experienced in the perpetual struggle between the desire for happiness (pleasure principle) and avoidance of pain (reality principle) often lead to neurosis and even psychosis. "Any attempt at rebellion (against society, i.e., reality) is seen (either) as psychosis," or "as a last technique of living, which will at least bring him substitutive satisfaction, (i.e.)...that of a flight into neurotic illness." Freud's concluding remark regarding the function of religion in this context is worth quoting:

> Religion restricts this play of choice and adaptation, since it imposes equally on everyone its own path to the requisition of happiness and protection from suffering. Its technique consists in depressing the value of life and distorting the picture of the real world in a delusional manner -- which presupposes an intimidation of the intelligence. At this price, by forcibly fixing them in a state of psychical infantilism and by drawing them into a mass-delusion, religion succeeds in sparing many people an individual neurosis. But hardly anything more. (pp. 31-32).

Why has mankind singularly, collectively, and consistently failed in his quest for happiness and the prevention of suffering? In attempting to answer this question, Freud says that a kind of "suspicion dawns on us" which says that maybe the answer lies in "a piece of our own psychical constitution." That is, the contention which "holds that what we call our civilization is largely responsible for our misery...(for) it is a certain fact that all the things with which we seek to protect ourselves against the threats that emanate from the sources of suffering are part of that very civilization (p. 33)."

Can it be? Civilization serves both to protect men against nature and to adjust their mutual relations. Wherein lies the evil, then? Certainly our civilization bore the culture from which came technical skills, fire and tool usage, writing and dwelling houses. And also, man invented gods to whom were attributed man's own cultural ideals. Furthermore, beauty, cleanliness and order became "requirements for civilization." And of all characteristics of civilization esteemed and encouraged most highly are man's higher mental activities, i.e., intellectual, scientific and artistic achievements, and "foremost among those ideas are the religious systems." The "motive force of all human activities," argues Freud, "is a striving towards the two confluent goals of utility and a yield of pleasure...(p. 41)."

The last and significantly problematic characteristic of civilization is the manner in which relationships of men to one another are regulated, i.e., family and state. "Human life in common," contends Freud, "is only made possible when a majority comes together which is stronger than any separate individual and which remains united against all separate individuals." Thus, a concept of the right or social good develops in opposition to individual brute force. "This replacement of the power of the individual by the power of a community constitutes the decisive step in civilization (p. 42)." The first requirement of this newly formed community is, therefore, justice -- the assurance that the good of the many expressed in law will be honored over the desires of any single individual. "The liberty of the individual is no gift of civilization." And in this connection, Freud would have us see that there is a great "similarity between the process of civilization and the libidinal development of the individual." As sublimation functions in the individual for the development of a strong ego and creative capacity to deal with the principle of reality, so likewise, "sublimation of instinct is an especially conspicuous feature of cultural development; it is what makes it possible for higher psychical activities, scientific, artistic or ideological, to play such an important part in civilized life (p. 44)."

As we move closer to Freud's perception of the nature of man in society -- man's stumbling futile attempts to construct a viable meaning to life -- we are confronted by an indispensable dialectic between life and death, especially as Freud had earlier developed the idea in his book, BEYOND THE PLEASURE PRINCIPLE (1920). He explains its development:

> There still remained in me a kind of conviction...that the instincts could not all be of the same kind...Starting from speculations on the beginning of life and from biological parallels, I drew the conclusion that, besides the instinct to preserve living substance and to join it into ever larger units, there must exist another, contrary instinct seeking to dissolve those units and to bring them back to their primordial, inorganic state. That is to say, as well as Eros there was an instinct of death (p. 66).

Within every society, as within every individual, there are two conflicting instincts. The life instinct is at the service of society so long as society is devoid of aggression, for aggression is a stark manifestation of the Death instinct. Aggression, says Freud, "is an original, self-subsisting instinctual disposition of man...(and it) constitutes the greatest impediment to civilization." Eros and Death share "world-dominion" and explain the movement of civilization back and forth upon the scale of creativity and destruction. This eternal and unexplainable struggle is essentially what life is all about, and the evolution of civilization is simply described "as the struggle for life of the human species." There is only futility in attempting to explain the meaning of life beyond this simple reality -- the meaning of life is the struggle of **life against death.** "And it is this battle of the giants," concludes Freud, "that our nurse-maids try to appease with their lullabies about Heaven (p. 69)."

It is the super-ego which constitutes the source of the human feelings of guilt. The super-ego evolves in consort with the development of the ego. As the ego gains relative control over the id, it does so by means of taking to itself the moral expectations of society, as society in turn, through the agency of parents, impresses its values upon the child. The super-ego is the projection of society's self-image into such an exalted state as to elicit devotion and adoration. But as the ego becomes educated to the reality principle, as a balancing source to the id's pleasure principle, the super-ego is being socially reinforced in the adoption of an ideal principle. As the ego's sense of reality confronts the super-ego's sense of the social ideal, tension results within the individual. The super-ego serves as the conscience which testifies against the ego's reluctance to support the ideals of society. "The tension between the harsh super-ego and the ego that is subjected to it," says Freud, "is called by us the sense of guilt; it expresses itself as a need for punishment (p. 70)." The stronger the ego, the weaker the super-ego, and vice versa. Society's moral expectations are mediated through the child's parents and give rise to a conscience educated to certain idealistic expectations. "Civilization, therefore," says Freud, "obtains mastery over the individual's dangerous desire for aggression by weakening and disarming it and by setting up an agency within him to watch over it..."

Guilt, which is really a social anxiety though frequently misnamed "bad conscience," often results from a "fear of loss of love" on the one hand and a "fear of punishment" on the other. But fundamentally, man's sense of guilt springs from the Oedipus complex "which was acquired at the killing of the father by the brothers banded together" as classically illustrated in Freud's scenario of the development of primeval human community in his TOTEM AND TABOO (1912). And thus, what began in relation to the father is completed in relation to the group. Freud reasons:

> If civilization is a necessary course of development from the family to humanity as a whole, then -- as a result of the inborn conflict arising from ambivalence, of the eternal struggle between the trends of love and death -- there is inextricably bound up with it an increase of the sense of guilt, which will perhaps reach heights that the individual finds hard to tolerate (p. 80).

It was Freud's intention from the beginning "to represent the sense of guilt as the most important problem in the development of civilization and to show that the price we pay for our advance in civilization is a loss of happiness through the heightening of the sense of guilt (p. 81)."

Quick to make a qualitative distinction between a "sense of guilt" and a "consciousness of guilt," Freud argues that guilt plays its greatest role in the human experience when operating in the unconscious. And when functioning here, "...the sense of guilt is at bottom nothing else but a topographical variety of anxiety; in its later phases it coincides completely with **fear of the super-ego** (p. 82)." To the extent that guilt remains unobserved in the dark chambers of the unconscious, man is condemned to writhe in his dissatisfaction -- a sort of **malaise** produced by civilization itself. "Religions," says Freud, "have never overlooked the part played in civilization by a sense of guilt." The sense of guilt, the harshness of the super-ego, the severity of the conscience -- all are demonstrative of a need for punishment. This need, says Freud, "is an instinctive (manifestation on the part of the ego) which has become masochistic under the influence of a sadistic super-ego..." Religion, as an illusion produced out of the imaginations of sublimated instincts, functions as a social neurosis which protects man from the stark realities of life devoid of any ultimate transcendent meaning. Mature men must eventually rid themselves of illusion and imagination and learn to face squarely and without guilt the meaninglessness of life.

Freud's attitude towards life's meaning is capsulated in a quotation from his study, CIVILIZATION AND ITS DISCONTENTS, with which we conclude our discussion:

> The fateful question for the human species seems to me to be whether and to what extent their cultural development will succeed in mastering the disturbance of their communal life by the human instinct of aggression and self-destruction...

> One thing only do I know for certain and that is that man's judgments of value follow directly his wishes for happiness -- that, accordingly, they are an attempt to support his illusions with arguments. (p. 92)

BIBLIOGRAPHIC NOTES

Sigmund Freud (1859-1939)

Biographical Sources

The definitive study of the life of Sigmund Freud, his personal history and the development of his thought, is that of Earnest Jones' LIFE AND WORK OF SIGMUND FREUD (1955), in three volumes. Being the authoritative source on Freud's life, it excels in its analysis of the ideo-cultural milieu within which Freud did his work. A very brief but excellent treatment of Sigmund Freud's life and thought for the beginning student who seeks a succinct introduction is found in Abraham Kardiner and Edward Preble's THEY STUDIED MAN (N.Y.: Mentor, 1963), Part II, "The New Dimension: Man," Chapter entitled, "Sigmund Freud: Chimney Sweeping."

Primary Sources

A definitive bibliography plus a substantial biography of Sigmund Freud is found in the ENCYCLOPEDIA OF THE SOCIAL SCIENCES. But for the student and scholar interested in a selection of Freud's works, particularly appropriate to our considerations here, one must begin with Freud's DIE TRAUMDETUNG, 1900 (trans., THE INTER-PRETATION OF DREAMS, London and N.Y., 1955, STANDARD EDITION, 4-5), which Freud considered his most important and scholar-ly work. This classic is an inquiry into the nature and function of the dream as it came to inform the entire psychoanalytic tradition.

Thirteen years later, Freud crashed into the world of religious specula-tion with his TOTEM AND TABU, Vienna, 1913 (trans., TOTEM AND TABOO, London, 1950; N.Y., 1952; STANDARD EDITION, 13, 1), which is a provocative and extremely controversial study of the individual psyche and extends the psychoanalytic method to the origins of society and culture. In this landmark study in psychology of religion, Freud traces the rise of the primal horde, its totemisms and incest taboos, the appearance and nature of guilt, and the basis of neurosis in the Oedipus complex. And, argues Freud, the origin of all religion, ethics, society, and art is in this primordial complex.

Because of the growing popularity of the psychoanalytic approach to mental health, and the increasing desire of many to understand it more fully, Freud was led to write VORLESUNGEN ZUR EIFUHRUNG IN DIE PSYCHOANALYSE, Vienna, 1916-1917 (trans., INTRODUCTORY LECTURES ON PSYCHO-ANALYSIS, London, 1929; A GENERAL INTRODUCTION TO PSYCHO-ANALYSIS, N.Y., 1935; Standard Edition, 15-16). This single work is a classic statement in clear and simple language of Freud's method of psychoanalysis. The book consists of 28 lectures to laymen and sets forth the fundamental theories of his system. Freud claimed that "the goal of all life is death," and in 1920, he explored this idea fully in his work entitled, JENSEITS DES LUSTPRINZIPS, Vienna, 1920, (trans., BEYOND THE PLEASURE PRINCIPLE, London, 1961; STANDARD EDITION, 18, 3). Freud contended that just as man is driven to seek pleasure, he is simultaneously obsessed with the imperative of death. For those seeking to understand the implications of this idea for life's meaning and purpose, this little book is a must.

The following year, Freud turned to the problems of the group and the individual ego, and wrote, MASSENPSYCHOLOGIE UND ICH-ANALYSE, Vienna, 1921 (trans., GROUP PSYCHOLOGY AND THE ANALYSIS OF THE EGO, London, 1959; N.Y., 1960; STANDARD EDITION, 18, 67). In this work, Freud offers clarification to old problems in understanding group behavior by means of his controversial theories of the ego, the unconscious, and the libido. The sequel to this study followed up the analysis of the origins and functions of the ego and the id, entitled, das ich und das es, Vienna, 1923 (trans., THE EGO AND THE ID, N.Y., 1961; STANDARD EDITION, 19, 3).

Freud's major statement, and sometimes considered his most controversial work, concerns the role of religion and faith in the development of the personality, society, and culture, and was suggestively entitled, DIE ZUKENFUT EINER ILLUSION, Vienna, 1927 (trans., THE FUTURE OF AN ILLUSION, London and N.Y., 1928; STANDARD EDITION, 21,3). Based on his clinical observations, Freud concluded that religion functioned as an infantile projection of the father as a means of forestalling the pressure of maturity and life's meaninglessness, i.e., religion was a sort of mass neurosis, "and not much more." Freud's DAS UNBEHAGEN IN DER KULTURE, Vienna (trans., CIVILIZATION AND ITS DISCONTENTS, London, 1930; N.Y., 1962; STANDARD EDITION, 21, 59) followed in 1930.

Freud's last entry into religious speculation, sometimes considered his worst study, sometimes his most stimulating, was entitled, DER MANN MOSES UND DIE MONOTHEISTISCHE RELIGION, 1939 (trans., MOSES AND MONOTHEISM, London and N.Y., 1939; Standard Edition, 23), and consisted of an inquiry into certain characteristics of the Jewish people in their relationship with Christians. Especially of significance was Freud's theory that Moses was an Egyptian and that the cherished memory his people had of him led to a monotheistic religion.

Secondary Sources

Over the past three decades, a mountain of literature cf varying quality has appeared in one form or another in response to Freud, e.g., Freudians, post-Freudians, neo-Freudians, anti-Freudians, etc. For the serious but uninitiated student of psychoanalytic theory, there are a few valuable sources which will serve as a point of beginning. No better treatment of Freud's theory exists in essay-form than that of Calvin S. Hall and Gardner Lindzey, entitled, "Freud's Psychoanalytic Theory," in their THEORIES OF PERSONALITY (N.Y.: John Wiley and Sons, 1967). In a collection of essays by such distinguished scholars Erik H. Erikson, Will Herberg, and Reinhold Niebuhr, Benjamin Nelson has edited a bock entitled, FREUD AND THE 20TH CENTURY (N.Y.: Meridian Bocks, 1957), which in a rather serious but brief manner surveys the impact Freud's thought has had upon such diverse fields of scholarship as "Philosophy and Religion," "Literature and the Arts," "Society and Politics," "The Sciences of Mind and Health." The late Deputy Director of the Institute of Social Psychiatry in London, Dr. James A. C. Brown, wrote a fine overview of the various schools of Freudians including whole chapters on such notables as Karen Horney, Erich Fromm, and Harry Stack Sullivan, entitled, FREUD AND THE POSTFREUDIANS (Baltimore: Penguin, 1969).

Two studies relating Freud's psychoanalytic theory to religion which are of particularly distinguishing scholarship are Philip Rieff's THE TRIUMPH OF THE THERAPEUTIC: USES OF FAITH AFTER FREUD (N.Y.: Harper Torchbock, 1968), and Peter Homans' THEOLOGY AFTER FREUD: AN INTERPRETIVE INQUIRY (N.Y.: Bobbs-Merrill, 1970), the latter being an attempt to construct an organic interpretation of Freud in dialogue with Niebuhr and Tillich. The single most controversial study of Freud's life and thought during the past decade is that by David Bakan, entitled, SIGMUND FREUD AND THE JEWISH MYSTICAL TRADITION (N.Y.: Schocken Books, 1969), in which

Bakan attempts, in a careful and scholarly manner, to place Freud within the mystical tradition of Judaism called Kabbalism. The furor this book has raised is evidence enough that it has much to offer the study of Freud, Judaism, and religion.

CHAPTER TWO

"After God"

"Man is nothing else but what he
makes of himself."

--Jean-Paul Sartre (1905-   )

Introduction

Here, we will consider a collection of brief essays by Jean-Paul
Sartre entitled, EXISTENTIALISM AND HUMAN EMOTIONS. Sartre,
propounding what he has chosen to label "atheistic existentialism,"
suggests that since "...God does not exist...there can be no human
nature..." and consequently the "first principle cf existentialism"
is simply that "Man is nothing else but what he makes of himself
-- what is called subjectivity..." Furthermore, the challenge of
modern man (called the experience of "forlornness") in the face
of the absence cf God, is to face all the consequences of this discovery. Therefore, after God, "Man is the future of man" and is
thus "condemned to be free" from the shackles of the Divine. The
question of meaning for Sartre is the question of how man can live
responsibly in a world "after God." Sartre pursues his question ruth-
lessly in these few essays.*

§ § §

Of the modern existentialists, few have had a wider range of impact
through both philosophical and literary writings than has the French-
man, Jean-Paul Sartre. Consistently inconsistent, Sartre first followed
this interest, then that interest, but wherever his thoughts have
taken him, he persists in his affirmation of man. Of those who affect-

---

*Unless otherwise noted, all quotations are from Sartre's EXISTEN-
TIALISM AND HUMAN EMOTION (1957).

ed his thought, such as his friends Albert Camus and Maurice Merleau-Ponty and such giants as Husserl and Heidegger, none had such pervasive impact upon Sartre as did Frederick Nietszche. In his novel, LA NAUSEE (1938) and in a collection of short stories, entitled, LE MUR (1939), Sartre lays out in elaborate and stark detail his perception of the predicament of man -- man "without excuse," "condemned to freedom," man "devoid of God." His most notable philosophical work, L'ETRE ET LA NEANT, 1943 (BEING AND NO-THINGNESS, 1956), was and is, without question, a profound piece of rigorous existentialist thought.

The discovery that "God does not exist," counsels Sartre, carries with it the necessity for man to face responsibly the "consequences" of life "after God." In true existentialist form, Sartre denies that there is a given nature of man. That is, Human Nature as a reality beyond the concept is a non-existent concoction of a philosophy seeking to escape the inevitabilities of a world devoid of Divine Will. Rather, in a world after God, man must learn to create for himself meaning and purpose. The essential character of reality is action, and in action man creates values for living from out of the meaninglessness of a godless world. The challenge for man is conceived in terms of a creative effort to live responsibly in a world devoid of **a priori** meaning and purpose, i.e., a world discovered and enduring "after God."

In a small collection of essays by Sartre, entitled, EXISTENTIALISM AND HUMAN EMOTION (1957), we have Sartre at his best and briefest. There is no substitute for reading his BEING AND NOTHINGNESS (1956) for a comprehensive exposure to his existential and phenomenological system in all its embellished finery. However, in our quest to come to terms with Sartre's understanding of life's meaning, no other collection of his profuse essay-writing equals the one here being considered.

Of singular excellence is the first essay entitled simply, "Existentialism." It is essentially a defense of Sartre's brand of existentialism "against some charges which have been brought against it." Critics of Sartre have observed that he is at his best in polemical writing and, indeed, this essay corroborates that view. The charges against existentialism come from a variety of rather diverse camps, especially from the Christians and the communists who have virtually nothing in common save a mutual dislike of Sartre and his philosophical thought. The communists, he points out amusingly, accuse him of a multitude of social evils, calling his philosophy "a kind of desperate quietism," "a philosophy of contemplation," "a bourgeois philosophy," and "pure subjectivity." On the other hand, the Christians charge him with inordinately "dwelling on human degradation" and with "pointing up everywhere the sordid, shady, and slimy, and neglecting the gracious and beautiful, the bright side of human nature...and (with) forgetting the smile of the child (p. 9)."

Of course the charges are wide-ranging and suggestive of deep ideological differences. Nevertheless, with resignation and no little self-confident optimism regarding the outcome of his response, he marches forward "to answer these different charges." From the very beginning, says Sartre, we must understand that by the term "existentialism we mean a doctrine which makes human life possible and, in addition, declares that every truth and every action implies a human setting and a human subjectivity (p. 10)." Sartre refuses to approach man from a philosophical anthropology which seeks to discover the nature of man. Man is action and subjectivity. Existentialism begins with man in the here and now of the immediate world environment, not in some abstracted Platonic Ideal or religious **imago de.**

Though existentialism "is regarded as something ugly" because it speaks of the "dark side of human life," Sartre is convinced that the real problem is the realization that man is, indeed, in a world devoid of supportive illusions. The intimidating and challenging message of existentialism is that "it leaves to man a possibility of choice (p. 12)." Of those who readily decry the "gloomy mood of existentialism," such catch phrases as "it's only human," "we should not struggle against the powers that be," and "we should not resist authority," all too easily foster a mood of resignation. Such a mood constitutes a veritable choice not to choose. Who, asks Sartre, ultimately is more gloomy? The citizen on the street who systematically opts outs of possible choice-making situations because of some childishly assumed cosmic plan or divine scheme, or the existentialist who recognizes that whatever meaning and purpose there is in life is a creation of man who chooses to act? The argument is well framed.

Though Sartre has defined existentialism above, he insists that beyond the definition lies a reality which must be characterized if existentialism is to be significantly and experientially grasped. Sartre derides those chic culturalists who so vaguely label everything from music and art to scandal and gossip as "existential." "Actually," argues Sartre, "existentialism is the least scandalous, the most austere of doctrines (p. 12)." A task intended strictly for the specialist and philosopher, existentialism is of two kinds: "Christian existentialism" as practiced by Jaspers and Marcel to mention only two among a host, and "atheistic existentialism" such as is done by Heidegger and the French existentialists not least of whom is Sartre himself. That common bond between these two branches is the belief "that existence precedes essence, or...that subjectivity must be the starting point (p. 13)." After God, i.e., after the discovery that the world is actually devoid of God, man must necessarily become the starting point.

In a world conceived theistically, i.e., God is Creator, "the individual man is the realization of a certain concept in the divine intelligence," and this is true whether one likes the theistic philosophical view of Descartes or that of Leibnitz (p. 14). Though devoid of an ostensibly theistic cosmology, nevertheless, the 18th century did support the "notion that essence precedes existence," and therefore, in Diderot, in Voltaire, and even in Kant, Man is understood as having a true nature. "This human nature...is found in all men, which means that each man is a particular example of a universal concept, man." Of all the great difficulties resultant from this kind of idealistic metaphysic, a simple one is seen in the difficulty with which Kant had to deal when lumping the "wild-man, the natural man, as well as the bourgeois" into the same human nature.

The incoherence, or near contradiction, of Christian existentialism becomes apparent when it says on the one hand that existence precedes essence while on the other claiming that God is. "Atheistic existentialism" claims Sartre, "is more coherent." In the absence of God, there is still one being in whom existence is first, namely in man. Man preceded the concept of man; he came before attempts to define his nature. Therefore, the existentialist must assert that "there is no human nature, since there is no God to conceive it (p. 15)." Man is freed from an **a priori** concept or definition of his being which precedes his actual life-experiences. Man now, "after God," is both what he "conceives himself to be" and "what he wills himself to be."

This discovery of man's existence devoid of any restricting predefined essence brings freedom, but also responsibility. Man must now "conceive" and "will" himself, or, in terms of the **first principle of existentialism,** "Man is nothing else but what he makes of himself." He is a plan aware of its own possibilities. After the demise of a confidence in a Heavenly Plan, Man comes face to face with his own subjectivity and immediacy of experience. And, because man exists before he is defined, man is responsible for the definition -- what he conceives and wills himself to be. "Thus," says Sartre to those who falsely accuse him of moral and social irresponsibility, "existentialism's first move is to make every man aware of what he is and to make the full responsibility of his existence rest on him (p. 16)."

This, says Sartre, is the fundamental challenge the existentialist calls forth, viz., the necessity of taking full cognizance of the fact that man alone is responsible for himself since God does not exist. This human subjectivity has a dual meaning: First, it means that every individual chooses and makes himself, and second, man is unable to transcend his own subjectivity. When men **choose**, they **affirm** the **value** of what they choose. And furthermore, since every individual chooses, affirms, and values at the same time, that which the individual chooses, "is valid for everybody and for our whole age (p. 17)." That is to say, in assuming responsibility for myself in a world after God, I am also choosing for all men. "In choosing myself," says Sartre, "I choose man," because "my action has involved all humanity." Those who accuse the existentialist of social irresponsibility have failed to understand the profound ethical imperative implicit in this necessity of individuals to "choose man."

Within the context of this imperative to assert oneself in a world devoid of **a priori** meaning and purpose, Sartre says we are better able to understand "what the actual content is" of such characteristic terms of the human condition as anguish, forlornness, and despair.

"Man is anguish" say the existentialists. He is so because, in a world after God wherein the individual must choose for himself and all mankind, he cannot "escape the feeling of his total and deep responsibility (p. 18)." And those people among us who disclaim anxiety about the human predicament are simply hiding their anxiety and fleeing it as a coward flees the battle. This anguish over man's condition characterizes all human experience, though it is seldom articulated and dealt with creatively. And though there be those who would seek quietism and passivity in the face of the existential demands to make choices in life, no one can truly escape, for not to choose is indeed to choose. Sartre says, for example, that all leaders know of this anguish because, as with all men, the demands to action necessitate a choice from a number of possibilities, all the while knowing that one's choice "has value only because it is chosen (p. 21)." Since there is no **a priori** ethic, man creates value by virtue of the choices he makes in the immediate situation. Anguish is the inevitable result of an awareness that choosing creates value in a world without essential goodness, only existential value.

From Heidegger, Sartre has taken the word "forlornness" and defines it as man's realization "that God does not exist and that we have to face all the consequences of this (p. 21)." Sartre is most critical of those secularizing ethicists who liberally profess the need to abolish God yet at minimal expense to society. They would dispose of God but cling to certain values to which they readily attribute **a priori** existence. Thus, social reform movements of a most simplistic sort often say essentially that "nothing will be changed if God does not exist." Sartre will have none of this liberalizing secularism!

"The existentialist, on the contrary," says Sartre, "thinks it very distressing that God does not exist (p. 22)," primarily because all hope of finding "values in a heaven of ideas" has consequently disappeared. There can no longer be a quest for an **a prior** God, since there is no "infinite and perfect consciousness to think it." Contrary to those liberalizing secularists who speak of a world unchanged by God's absence, Sartre quotes Dostoyevsky in support of atheistsic existentialism, who has said: "If God didn't exist, everything would be possible." This, says Sartre, "is the very starting point of existentialism." The experience of forlornness derives from the realization that man "can't start making excuses for himself," that in essence, he is "condemned to be free." He is condemned because he did not create himself, yet free because he is responsible for the way he conceives and wills himself and all other men to be. Quoting Ponge, Sartre says that, consequently, "Man is the future of man." Condemnation and freedom go hand in hand -- condemned to life, free to act. "Forlornness and anguish go together," explains Sartre, for "forlornness implies that we ourselves choose our being and anguish implies an existential awareness of the human condition devoid of **a priori** foundations (p. 29)."

Despair is the third characteristic of the human situation. Simply stated, despair "means that we shall confine ourselves to reckoning only with what depends upon our will, or on the ensemble of probabilities which make our action possible (p. 29)." Or, in the words of Descartes, "Conquer yourself rather than the world." Man is what he wills himself to be. Action results from this will, and the moment the possibilities being considered become disassociated from an imperative to action (decision-making and follow-through), Sartre says we must disengage ourselves. Man must limit himself to what he sees, to situations wherein he can act. "Actually," says Sartre, "things will be as man will have decided they are to be (p. 31)." The result of such a posture is not quietism, but action informed by a will to choose from among various options tempered with the realities of ever-present risk. First, says Sartre, "I should involve myself (and should) act on the old saying, 'Nothing ventured -- nothing gained.'" Quietism is a doctrine which lets others do what I think I cannot do or what I fear to do. The ethic of existentialism runs diametrically opposite to quietism. An existential ethic declares: "There is no reality except in action," and furthermore, it contends that "Man is nothing else than his plan; he exists only to the extent that he fulfills himself; he is therefore nothing else than the ensemble of his acts, nothing else than his life (p. 32)."

Though this view may and does horrify people, it is really the inevitable results of the discovery of man's true situation as being alone in the world. In trying to cope with one's wretchedness, the easy way out is to blame one's condition on circumstances beyond one's control. For those who aspire (without will and action) to greatness, whether in art, literature, music, scholarship or whatever, and fail to realize their wistful dreams, the existentialist offers no comfort. To blame failure on outside circumstances is bad faith, and demonstrably infantile. There is no genius other than that which is "manifest" and "expressed." "A man is involved in life, leaves his impress on it, and outside of that there is nothing (p. 33)." What foolishness to speak of what might have been! "Reality alone is what counts, (for) dreams, expectations, and hopes warrant no more than to define a man as a disappointed dream, as miscarried hopes, as vain expectations." The existentialist will not define man in such negative resignation, but rather positively -- "You are nothing else than your life." To label the existentialist pessimistic, then, is to misperceive his true character, viz., as one of "optimistic toughness."

Existentialism, rid of restrictive and ofttimes debilitating **a priori** categories of idealistic metaphysics, "defines man in terms of action;" its ethic is an "ethic of action." The existentialist seeks to establish a "doctrine based on truth and not (on) a lot of fine theories full of hope but with no real bases." There is only one real truth, and that is the Cartesian **cogito: I think, therefore, I exist.** There is no universal essence and no universal human nature, but there is undeniably "a universal human condition (p. 38)." Though history and geography vary, what does not vary is the necessity for man, all men in all times and places, "to exist in the world, to be at work there, to be there in the midst of other people, and to be mortal there." By this line of reasoning which says that a single individual experience of whatever sort is analogous to the whole human condition at all times and places, Sartre is led to say that, whether speaking of Chinese, Africans, Indians, or Frenchmen, "every configuration (i.e., experiential situation) has universality in the sense that every configuration can be understood by every man." In this sense, the existentialist can speak of a universality of the human situation and though not given, "it is perpetually being made (p. 39)."

In the arena of the universality of experience, man is forced to make choices which affirm human value. No one is exempt from decision-making. "In one sense," says Sartre, "choice is possible, but what is not possible is not to choose (p. 41)." And, since the choice is freely made from among a variety of supposedly equally viable possibilities, ethical decisions can be compared to the "making of a work of art." The analogy between ethical choices and aesthetic values is a good one, because with both there is no **a priori**. What art and ethics have in common, in a world after God and thus devoid of a heavenly plan, is the qualities of "creation and invention." "Man makes himself (p. 43)," says Sartre, and consequently, both art and ethics are his creation and his invention. And, reasons Sartre, since "we define man only in relationship to involvement," aesthetics and ethics are possible only as man engages them in his creative and inventive activities.

Recognizing that human depravity must allow for the possibility that some men will choose dishonestly, Sartre says that the existentialist is not in a position to pass moral judgment upon dishonest decisions since there are no **a priori** ethical standards. Nevertheless, the existentialist can label dishonesty as error. Dishonesty is a falsehood because it essentially undermines the possibility of "complete freedom of involvement." Just as there is dishonesty in a choice made as if freedom was not absolute, so likewise, Sartre considers as dishonest the position which claims "that certain values exist prior to me...(p. 45)." Complete freedom of involvement implies, even demands, that decisions be made without reliance either upon supposed **a priori** ethical categories or upon an intentional limiting of the range of possibilities. Therefore, says Sartre, "...the ultimate meaning of the acts of honest men (i.e., those who accept neither universal givens nor arbitrary limitations of possibilities) is the quest for freedom as such."

Honest men seek freedom. But freedom for oneself implies freedom for all at the point at which I myself become involved in the pursuit of freedom. That is, as I take freedom as my own personal goal,

I do so only by recognizing that I take freedom as the goal of all men. In the context of the recognition of and participation in the "universality of the human situation," the existentialist realizes that the desire for personal freedom is simultaneously a desire for the freedom of all humanity.

Furthermore, and most importantly for the development of an existential ethic, I must face responsibly the realization that as I choose freedom for myself, and thus for all men, I must necessarily pass judgment upon those who for whatever reason choose to hide themselves from the "complete arbitrariness" and the "complete freedom" offered them in their existence. This is true whether they hide by means of allegiance to a supposedly universal code or by means of intentionally narrowing their range of possible choices. Sartre puts his views this way:

> Those who hide their complete freedom from themselves out of a spirit of seriousness or by means of deterministic excuses, I shall call cowards; those who try to show that their existence was necessary, when it is the very contigency of man's appearance on earth, I shall call stinkers (p. 46).

The content of ethics is relative, says Sartre, but the form of ethics is universal, and that universal is **man choosing freedom.** Ethics are mature and responsible to the degree that they seek out and are made in the name of freedom. And, it must necessarily follow, since values are relative (though their impetus is universal, viz., the human quest for freedom), "values aren't serious, since you choose them." Though "I'm quite vexed that that's the way it is," says Sartre, nonetheless, he reasons, "if I've discarded God the Father, there has to be someone to invent values (p. 49)." There we have it. In the name of complete freedom of involvement, in a world after God wherein neither cowards nor stinkers have status, the existentialist must come to terms with his anguish, his despair, and his forlornness. This is done by asserting oneself responsibly in the creation and invention of ethical and aesthetical values. "You've got to take things as they come," counsels Sartre.

In this context, Sartre assails a wrong-headed kind of humanism which, as in the cult of mankind propounded by Auguste Comte, for example, "ascribes a value to man on the basis of the highest deeds of certain men." This kind of pseudo-humanism Sartre considers absurd. Another more responsible conception of humanism is exemplified by the existentialist. This kind of existentialistic humanism reminds man that there is no law-maker but himself, that he must decide alone, and that his liberation from forlornness will result from his decision to seek outside of himself the goal of freedom. "Existentialism," explains Sartre, "is nothing else than an attempt to draw all the consequences of a coherent atheistic position (p. 51)." With regard to the human necessity of creating values in a world after God, Sartre says by way of concluding his essay:

> Moreover, to say that we invent values means nothing else but this: life has no meaning **a priori.** Before you come alive, life is nothing; it's up to you to give it a meaning, and value is nothing else but the meaning that you choose. (p. 49).

BIBLIOGRAPHICAL NOTE

Jean-Paul Sartre (1905–   )

Biographical Sources

Two significant full-length biographies of Sartre's life have appeared which merit mentioning here. The earlier and more balanced appreciation of Sartre as philosopher and man of letters is Iris Murdoch's SARTRE: ROMANTIC RATIONALIST (New Haven, 1953), but of enlightening worth is Mary Warnock's analytical philosopher's view of Sartre, entitled, THE PHILOSOPHY OF SARTRE (London, 1965). A brief sketch of his life and work can, of course, be found in the DICTIONARY OF PHILOSOPHY.

Primary Sources

Sartre's writings are naturally divisible into those which are overtly philosophical and those which are obviously literary. We must say "overtly" because all of Sartre's writings, however classified, speak out of his existentialism. Few thinkers have so well integrated their philosophical outlook with their literary work as has Sartre. The following are samples of his novels, plays, and literary essays: LA NAUSEE, Paris, 1938 (trans. by Lloyd Alexander as NAUSEA, N.Y., 1949); REFLEXIONS SUR LA QUESTION JUIVE, Paris, 1946 (trans. by George J. Becker as ANTI-SEMITE AND JEW, N.Y., 1948); BAUDELAIRE, Paris, 1947 (trans. by Martin Turnell under the same title, Norfolk, Ct., 1950); HUIS CLOS and LES MOUCHES, in Theatre, Vol. I, Paris, 1947 (trans. by Stuart Gilbert as NO EXIST and THE FLIES, in TWO PLAYS, N.Y., 1947); LE DIABLE ET LE BON DIEU, Paris, 1952 (trans. by Kitty Black as LUCIFER AND THE LORD, London, 1952); SAINT GENET: COMEDIEN ET MARTYRE, Paris, 1952 (trans. by Bernard Frechtman as SAINT GENET: ACTOR AND MARTYR, N.Y., 1963). The student who would like to read what is the undisputed classic in existential literature should read Sartre's short story, entitled, LE MUR, translated by Lloyd Alexander under the title, THE WALL (New Directions, 1948).

Sartre's philosophical career began with the appearance of an essay entitled, "La Transcendance de L'Ego," in RECHERCHES PHILOSO-PHIQUES, vol. VI (1936), 65-123 (trans. by Forrest Williams and Robert Kirkpatrick as THE TRANSCENDENCE OF THE EGO, N.Y., 1937), which was Sartre's beginning and somewhat tentative entry into the world of psychoanalytic theory. He soon followed up the theme with a book on emotions, entitled, ESQUISSE D'UNE THEORIE DES EMOTIONS, Paris, 1939 (trans. by Bernard Frechtman as THE EMOTIONS: OUTLINE OF A THEORY, N.Y., 1948; and trans. by Philip Mairet as SKETCH FOR A THEORY OF THE EMOTIONS, London, 1962). Sartre's existentialism was beginning to bloom and this study struck a motif which would follow throughout his career.

The following year, Sartre came forth with a phenomenological inquiry into the nature of man's imagination from the point of view of existential psychology, entitled, L'IMAGINAIRE: PSYCHOLOGIE PHENOMENOLOGIQUE DE L'IMAGINATION, Paris, 1940 (trans. by Bernard Frechtman as THE PSYCHOLOGY OF IMAGINATION, N.Y., 1948). Without question, Sartre's most scholarly and internationally recognized philosophical treatise is, L'ETRE ET LE NEANT: ESSAI D'ONTOLOGIE PHENOMENOLOGIQUE, Parish, 1943 (trans. by Hazel E. Barnes as BEING AND NOTHINGNESS, N.Y. 1956).

Throughout his writings, and particularly in this work, Sartre dealt with the fundamental problem of dualism, i.e., subject and object, as perceived between the subjective consciousness and objective Being, including such problems as the relationship between the subjective experience of freedom and the experience of the objective **thing. Being** refers to Sartre's rendition of the Kantian thing-in-itself or the Hegelian Absolute, whereas **Nothingness** refers to the structure of the individual object which Sartre identifies as **Freedom.** Since the appearance of this major work, Sartre has spent his time developing, re-defining, and defending its basic positions.

His more important subsequent writings include L'EXISTENTIALISME EST UN HUMANISME, Paris, 1946 (trans. by Philip Mairet as EX-ISTENTIALISM AND HUMANISM, London, 1948); SITUATIONS I AND III, Paris, 1947, 1949 (two volumes of philosophical and literary essays). The two most important essays in these collections are "La Liberte Cartesienne," and "Materialisme et Revolution," both of which have been translated by Annette Michelson in LITERARY AND PHILOSOPHICAL ESSAYS, N.Y., 1955; and QUESTIONS DE METHODE and CRITIQUE DE LA RAISON DIALECTIQUE, vol. I, Paris, 1960 (trans. by Hazel E. Barnes as THE PROBLEM OF METHOD, London, 1964).

Secondary Sources

Several excellent accounts of the work of Sartre exist, but some with more perspective than others, e.g., A. J. Ayer has written a fine but highly critical estimation of Sartre as a philosopher from an analytical philosopher's perspective, entitled,"Novelist-Philosophers: J. P. Sartre," HORIZON, XII (1945), 12-26, 101-110. Wilfred Desan has written a careful explication of some central themes of Sartre's ontology in THE TRAGIC FINALE (Cambridge, Mass., 1954), and Francis Jeason has written what is generally considered the best treatment of the ethical aspects of Sartre's philosophy in LE PROBLEME MORALE ET LA PENSEE DE SARTRE (Paris, 1947), Sartre himself writing the Preface.

An excellent essay on Sartre's phenomenology including a detailed bibliography was written by Herbert Spiegelberg, entitled, "The phenomenology of Jean-Paul Sartre," in THE PHENOMENOLOGICAL MOVEMENT, two volumes (The Hague, 1960), vol. II, Chapter 10. Two short but helpful essays on Sartre in the context of other 19th and 20th century existentialists such as Kierkegaard, Nietzsche, and Maritain appear in H. J. Blackham's SIX EXISTENTIALIST THINKERS (N.Y.: Harper and Row, 1959), and in Paul Ramsey's NINE MODERN MORALISTS (Englewood Cliffs, N.Y.: Prentice-Hall, Inc., 1962).

CHAPTER THREE

"Within the Void"

"A culture comes into being and endures through
its ability to create a myth. The experience of
nothingness is the origin of all myth making. . .
Culture begins and ends in the void."

--Michael Novak (1933-   )

Introduction

Michael Novak has only lately come into the fray to wrestle with
the problem of meaning, but his work is already laying claim to
the serious attention of notable scholars such as Charles Frankel,
Bernard J. F. Lonergan, and Krister Stendahl. In Novak's THE EX-
PERIENCE OF NOTHINGNESS, considered in this chapter, the
question of meaning is posed in an existentialistic frame of reference,
contending that of late modern man has had to face for the first
time the experience of stark nothingness. Mediated through the
experiences of boredom, helplessness, betrayal, drugs and rootlessness,
the experience of nothingness has finally broken through our self-
protective shield of progress, pragmatism, and fulfillment. "No
man has a self or an identity...," says Novak, and therefore "he must
constantly be **inventing** selves." As a "mode of consciousness," the
experience of nothingness is "a kind of exhaustion of spirit that
comes from seeking 'meaning' too long and too ardently." And yet,
says Novak, the "experience of nothingness is the origin" of all culture
because "culture begins and ends in the void." Novak's concern is
for modern man to learn to live within the void out of which an
existential ethic can emerge, for, says he, "...there is never any
excuse for man, never."*

§ § §

---

*Unless otherwise noted, all quotations are from Novak's THE EXPER-
IENCE OF NOTHINGNESS (1970).

Michael Novak is the youngest and latest modern thinker to be considered in this study. Nevertheless, the impact his thought is beginning to have in Western culture, especially in American circles, is demonstrative of his clear perception and captivating analysis of modern man's search for meaning. Since the mid-sixties, he has kept the publishers busy with provocative and ofttimes controversial works on subjects ranging from marriage and middle-class values to politics, theology and ethnic studies. But whatever the topic, there is an underlying continuity to his thought, and without doubt, his recent book, entitled, THE EXPERIENCE OF NOTHINGNESS, displays in a fine manner the continuity in his perception of the American experience.

Of those extolling the merit of Novak's thought today, Charles Frankel of BOOK WORLD has called him "a philosopher of the rising generation," and Wayne Saffen of the NATIONAL CATHOLIC REPORTER has suggested that Novak's "book may be judged great." Two prominent Harvard theologians have not failed to speak of Novak's importance, Bernard Lonergan calling him "an articulate and incisive thinker," and Krister Stendahl confessing, "I was moved by this book -- not only by its honesty, but by the way that honesty vibrates with tenderness." To have lumped Novak in the company of such undisputed giants as Freud, Heschel, and Barth may be considered a bit presumptuous, but in light of the immediate search for meaning and the frequent experience of nothingness which often results from the quest, Novak seems to have spoken to both the search and the experience in such timely and challenging ways as to validate his place in our study. Whether he will stay among this company of giants is for history to tell, but at least for now, it appears that Novak is a welcomed guest at the table of greatness.

After the Bomb, after Bangladesh, after Vietnam, after Watergate -- we have all "seen too much" and have all "absorbed too much pain," says Novak, "to go on believing in mirages." After the shallow and fleeting joys of success, progress, and advancement, we finally and inevitably come face to face with "the dizzy inner spaces of our rootlessness." No longer can we muster great excitement about the future, no longer can we gather the crowds to cheer the march of progress -- hope is gone, and we are stronger for it. "Our hope," says Novak, "is an acceptance of despair." The insanity and vanity of it all -- that great American Dream of never-ending advancement, progress, success -- how tragically we have been its victim now forced to face the consequences. Anguish-Forlornness-Despair -- these are the by-words of a materialistic, ethnocentric society come of age. But what to do now? This is Novak's primary concern. "Granted that I have the experience of nothingness," says Novak, "what shall I do with it?"

There are those who would say nothing is left but despair, nothing left but meaninglessness. In the words of Dostoyevsky, "Suicide (becomes) the ultimate expression of freedom." Indeed, Novak will concede that in a world where the experience of nothingness is so pervasive as to make talk of meaning and purpose to life seem weirdly out of place, he is not quite ready to reason that because "the possibilities are limitless" that there is no legitimate motive to act, to become involved, to will. "I want to unmask one piece of ideology only," pleads Novak, and that is "that the experience of nothingness necessarily incapacitates one from further action (p.ix)." Novak so completely succeeds in making the experience of nothingness seem so genuinely and honestly characteristic of our own time and our own society that to contend in the face of such a profoundly debilitating and demoralizing experience that we are not left helpless and eternally doomed to inaction is, indeed, a great contention. However, he does not shrink from the challenge to discover a context for action, a foundation for ethics, a cornerstone for values, within the realities of the experience of nothingness, that is, "within the void."

Though the point will appear frequently in this investigation, nevertheless, let it be registered initially that for Novak, the experience of nothingness is not to be moved beyond or left behind as we attempt to find a place to build an ethic. Rather, whatever meaning and purpose to life there are to be discovered after the coming of the experience of nothingness, it is from within the void that they must arise. Only when we understand that Novak's existentialism begins where Sartre's leaves off can we come to grips with Novak's search for meaning. that is, within the realization that life is essentially meaningless and only existentially is it possible to create purpose and value, there must, nevertheless, be certain ingredients indigenous to the immediacy of our experience together here and now which, if perceived and creatively used, can give rise to an ethic upon which our life together can dwell responsibly.

Novak's work being considered here is divided into four short chapters. The first two are essentially descriptive of the experience of nothingness, the second two are explorations of the implications of the experience of nothingness for ethical responsibility. Let us first try to come to an understanding of this experience of nothingness, and then seek out its ethical possibilities.

There is no human nature, only separate natures of men; no true individuated self, only fleeting moments of personal identity. That we all have a common nature and that we all have a genuine separateness to ourselves, called "I", is a falsehood propagated by a society which simultaneously values group unity and strong individuated selves. A consumer-oriented society which demands hard work from its constituency must traffic in the rhetoric of individualism while also praising the team spirit. Not only is the self a society-serving mythical creation perpetrated for its own aggrandizement, but so are all the social institutions which are "designed to hold chaos and formlessness at bay..." The American culture has created a myth which permeates every symbol of its corporate life, the three-layered myth of **progress-pragmatism-fulfillment.** And up until the middle of this century, the myth functioned well. The Great American Dream -- the myth of progress -- served well a young nation of people seeking to make a place for themselves, seeking a place at the head of the march of nations. America was on the move -- baseball, hot dogs, apple pie, and Chevrolets became the sacred symbols of this dauntless society. America was waking up to cornflakes, drinking Coke at the county fair, making bigger, better, and more of whatever could be called "new and improved." And for those who were not actually living the dream, they were dreaming the dream. With hard work, clean living, a course from Dale Carnegie and a prayer from Norman Vincent Peale, anyone could advance in the "Land of Opportunity."

And then, about a decade or so ago, the myth began to develop some holes in it. America began to remember the Bomb, we found out that some Americans, in spite of hard work and clean living, were not advancing. We learned that guns can't change an Oriental's heart grasped by a vision of a communal world, that "the system" too often was selfserving. No part of American Society was exempt. As hard as we tried, happiness did not easily come and never lingered long. The myth from which we had come was beginning to show signs of decay. And the harder we worked to keep it fresh -- e.g., with slogans like "America, Love It or Leave It" -- the more rapidly decay took over. "The experience of nothingness in America," observes Novak, "cuts across all networks...(and) the sense of security has been undermined...(for) the experience of nothingness seeps into our awareness through a sieve (p. 6)." We must now passionately defend what once was so universally accepted -- "Progress" is now accused of being nothing more than a euphemism for "Imperialism."

The experience of nothingness is upon us. It is not on the horizon of America; it is on the backs and in the hearts of her citizens. And no one is exempt from its grip. "Boredom," says Novak, "is the first taste of nothingness." With the "discovery that everything is a game," men lose the passion for action. With the discovery that Elmer Gantry is less pious and more potent than he should be, that Superman wears arch supports, that kids cheat in the National Soapbox Derby -- life becomes a game with loosely defined rules and disinterested players. Sleep and pills, suicide and television all become agencies of escape. No longer is "time of the essence," for progress and advancement have lost their charm. "Killing time" has become a way of life of those in the grips of the experience of nothingness.

"Besides boredom," says Novak, "there is the collapse of a strongly inculcated set of values (p. 7)." With the decline of an all-seeing Eye who consistently is on the side of parents, society, law and order, there is a resulting loss of a sense of ethical fundamentals. Morality becomes an exceedingly relative business, and situationalism is taken for granted. Those seeking safety within the storm join fanatical religious sects or run off to communal farms in Maine. With both God and the Devil disposed of, society becomes the Devil and the social outcast becomes God. The Devil resides in Washington, D.C., and God lurks about the natural food store. The quest for security in social radicalism or communal living is, nevertheless, the futile attempt of irresponsible cowards fleeing the onslaught of nothingness. Both liquor and pills, television and stereo, the Cadillac and the chopper are all unsuccessful attempts to escape.

Furthermore, within the void one feels completely helpless. The radical rhetoric to the contrary notwithstanding, this feeling of help-lessness is not political. Who could watch the Watergate trials, observing the faces of both the defendants and prosecutors, and not see a bone-deep helplessness in bold relief? Not only do I not have power over my own life, but society seems singularly devoid of anyone who does. And not only do men feel helpless, there is also a sense of "be-trayal by permissiveness, pragmatism, and value-neutral discourse (p. 8)." For those who have loyally adhered to the great ideals of American Society, who have voted regularly, paid their taxes, supported charitable organizations, and worked for better schools, they now find out that they have been betrayed by corrupt government, inequit-able tax scales, embezzlement and fraud from charitable organizations, and school policy-makers who prefer politics to quality education. And, with this experience of betrayal comes a **laissez-faire** attitude among the elders and a "Do your own thing" attitude among America's youth. Sunshine and orange juice will not set a society aright when its sincere and dedicated constituents feel bored, helpless, and betrayed.

Having first tasted nothingness in boredom, we come full turn into its spell with the drug culture, rootlessness, and sexual promiscuity. Drugs can take you high, they can take you low, make you smile, make you cry, help you sleep, help you stay awake, make you eat, make you diet, make you feel no pain, or bring you death. Drugs can do it all except bring you meaning and purpose in life. And furthermore, of all the symbols of American culture which carry significance for its citizens, the drugstore and moving van are probably the most recognized. Certainly these symbols are worshipped by the masses in need of a faith equal to their doubts and fears. Whereas drugs will do for you what you want where you are, the moving van offers hope and advancement in a new way of life in a new location. The moving van is to contemporary America what the covered wagon was to the American pioneer, with one notable exception. The pioneer, moving ever westward, dreamed of a limitless expanse of virgin land awaiting his plows and posts, whereas the modern American travels in irregular circles, exchanging places with the fellow just before him who shared the same empty dreams of advancement and happiness. Unlike the view from the buckboard seat, the view from the cab of a tractor-trailer truck soon brings boredom and drowsiness.

And if pills and wheels have not sufficiently devastated the American morale, the deterioration of sex **mores** certainly has. In an earlier day, when our myth was well and thriving, romance was everywhere sought and universally valued. Whether dancing with Fred Astaire, singing with Doris Day, or fighting with Humphrey Bogart, love and romance were there in full bloom romanticism. Now romance has gone and "funky" has come. Imagination and fantasy are gone, nudity and debauchery are here. In speaking of sexuality, Novak says: "It comes too cheaply: its intimacy is mainly fake; its symbolic power is reduced to the huddling warmth of kittens in the darkness -- not to be despised, but open as a raw wound to the experience of nothingness (p. 9)." The once cherished image of the lover has been reduced to that of the bunk-buddy. Nowhere is the experience of nothingness more prevalant or more starkly displayed than in the contemporary cinema. Who can sit through "The Godfather," "Deep Throat," or "Bonnie and Clyde" and not feel the icy hands of nothingness upon one's shoulder? And though television tries to offer the old myth in new dress with such faint-hearted and sentamental programs as "Apple's Way," "The Waltons," and "Little House on the Prairie," the myth is dying all the same.

The experience of nothingness as a "mode of human consciousness" is exemplified in such a question as: "Does death make any difference?" In a time when God is felt to be near, the challenge to man is not in living creatively, but in dying meaningfully. But in a time after God and within the void, the challenge is how to live meaningfully and die with dignity. The experience of nothingness, Novak would have us believe, is "a kind of exhaustion of spirit that comes from seeking 'meaning' too long and too ardently (p. 11)." The structures of our life, particularly that of the individuated ego and that of society, are constructed so as to guard us from the void and meaninglessness which crouch just outside the walls of self and state. And yet, when reason breaks down and the walls begin to crack, the experience of nothingness patiently but doggedly awaits our irrational outbursts.

Then and there, says Novak, the experience of nothingness "arises near the borderline of insanity." And even though those who have been brought up properly have "been sheltered from the experience of nothingness," nevertheless, "the source of the experience of nothingness lies in the deepest recesses of human consciousness, in its irrepressible tendency to ask questions (p. 14)." It is precisely at this juncture, where the experiencer of nothingness begins to ask questions, that a new beginning may be discovered. From within the void, a new myth may arise bringing with it a new culture and a new experience.

Quoting approvingly from Albert Camus who said, "Even within nihilism, it is possible to find the means to proceed beyond nihilism," Novak makes a contention that men are free, even condemned to freedom, and this freedom requires responsible action. "Exactly in proportion as we are free men," reasons Novak, "we are responsible for the social, economic, and political practices of our nation...(p. 16)." But true ethical responsibility arising out of freedom is inevitably at odds with the culture from which it springs, for freedom and responsibility, when taken seriously, conflict with the established values of culture. As the experience of nothingness is born within the context of a culture whose myth is vanishing, so the freedom which grows within nothingness must contrast the values of its parent culture. When that which one has taken as reality (my culture, my values, my goals) begins to be perceived as myth, then my culture, my values, my goals become useless relativities of a formless and directionless life. The scenario of culture-death and re-birth proceeds like this:

> A culture comes into being and endures through its ability to create a myth. The experience of nothingness is the origin of all myth making. Is it any wonder that every myth leads back to that primal experience? Culture begins and ends in the void. An honest culture does not evade its origin or its end. (p. 23)

As man is devoid of any universal nature or any truly individuated self, so he must construct for himself each day and in each place a plan of action. And since his recent discovery, by way of the experience of nothingness, that social institutions and social rules are in reality only mythical devices to perpetuate the **status quo**, he must assert his creative ingenuity in designing a plan of action by which to live. This plan of action Novak calls "story." "The story a man is acting out determines his actions more than the verbally stated rule he is following (p. 24)." So, not only must man create a game-plan, but also the game-plan in a real sense must create man. All men act upon their own personal story as their own story acts upon them. "Human acts," explains Novak, "...have a base in myth; there is no human act that is not an acting out of a story (p. 26)."

But, if our actions are based on stories which are spun of mythical thread, how can we expect to act responsibly, where is the foundation for an ethic? In order to explain his theory of existential ethics which affirms both freedom to act and responsibility to act, Novak suggests the visual image of an "horizon." "An horizon," explains Novak, "has two poles: the subject (man), and the range of his activities." I am the subject and the possibilities for any specific action constitutes my range. Since what we know of the world is an all pervasive interpenetration of "self" and "world." The pole of subjectivity, "I", is characterized by the activities of "experiencing, understanding, evaluating, and doing," whereas the pole of objectivity, "Culture," constitutes a range of institutions -- family, school, church, state, etc. These two interpenetrating poles establish between themselves an horizon upon which or along which decisions must daily be made.

Because man is both a question-asker and a symbol-maker, he is capable of "orderly and intellectually manageable development." But, "the concept of horizon is intended," contends Novak, "to pierce the rationalistic bias by calling attention to the fundamental role of undifferentiated, inexhaustible experience." Therefore, the responsibility implied in this theory is that, given the presence of the experience of nothingness, we must become "consciously aware of -- and appropriate -- our own actual horizons." Gone is the stability of a world wherein the culture-legacy of establishing values is lost, all things become relative, all things situational. This flux is the experience of nothingness, and furthermore, "it is the task of ethical reflection today to make such formlessness its starting place (p. 29)."

Before we can explore more programmatically the development of an existential ethic from within the void, we must explore a bit more the source of nothingness and the situations within which it arises. "The experience of nothingness," explains Novak, "arises when I discover that my myth is not necessary and inescapable, but arbitrary and socially prearranged (p. 30)." And though this experience and this discovery motivates me to seek a more "accurate version of reality," my search leads, on the contrary, to the realization that the alternatives are equally arbitrary. However, for those remaining Americans who hold to the myth of advancement and herald the progress of science, research, and technology, "the experience of nothingness is a childish indulgence." To these individuals, found in fanatical religious groups, political left organizations and liberal culture the experience of nothingness "is symptomatic of a sick, perverse loss of nerve." These society drop-outs, they contend, believe it is "more true that the world is so absurd that only the insane are in tune with it," and this fate is designed for those who would lose faith in the American Dream.

But this kind of optimism, says Novak, is short-lived and brings tragedy and despair in its wake. The three-pillared temple of realism, pragmatism, and empiricism built upon the three-layered foundation of Pierce, James, and Dewey is crumbling. Those who worship here are the ones who have a loss of nerve, they are the ones who flee the encroaching nothingness of a life within the void. The laboratory, the test-tube the launching-pad are so blatantly "matter-of-fact, automatic, and functional" as to deride the possibility of "reverence, metaphysical wonder, and sense of mystery" in the world. "Objectivity in short," accuses Novak, "has the logical status of a myth...(p. 27)."

And so long as men refrained from asking questions, the myth worked. America progressed. We advanced. We developed. We overcame our adversaries from within and without. But, when the discovery was made that there are no "facts out there" and "interpretation in here," rather only people choosing to observe and act upon arbitrarily selected data, the myth of objectivity lost its captivating power. Men began to understand in terms of "a new sense of reality" which says that "scholarly projects have social and political implications," and the image of a white-coated scientist, sterilized laboratory, and objective experimentation is exposed as ludicrous.

The experience of nothingness arising out of the discovery of the culture-myth results from man's propensity to question. "The drive to question," says Novak, "is a fundamental tendency and vital force of the human personality (p. 47)." And with the asking of questions, cultures appear and cultures crumble. The mythical response to the asking of questions forestalls disaster for only a moment, for when the myth which culture puts forth in answer to questions is scrutinized, its strength to hold society together weakens, arbitrariness moves in, fear encroaches, despair reigns. This spiralling dialectical tension of asking questions gives rise, finally, to a uniquely human feeling, namely, anxiety. The drive to question leads down the road to anxiety, the components of which, says Novak, are "helplessness and loneliness," and "its terminus is the perception of one's own death." As noted earlier, the challenge to modern man is not how to die, but rather, in a world after God and thus within the void, the perception of one's own death sets the stage for the crucial challenge of the age, **"Granted that I must die, how shall I live?** (p. 48)."

The experience of nothingness brings with it the intimidation of culturally-pat answers to simplistic questions, and with the deterioration of the old culture and its supportive myths comes the on-slaught of new questions which only a new culture with new myths can address. The question of how to live, stimulated by the experience of nothingness, is, according to Novak, "the fundamental human question, which," says he, "fundamental myths aim to answer." Man as symbol-maker has an uncanny capacity to take poor tools and turn them into profound carriers of his existential meaning. Yet, symbols, because they are particularized expressions of immediate experiences, are selective in their range of expressions and distortive in their conveyance of experiences. Therefore, says Novak, "of the two drives (to ask questions and make symbols), the drive to question seems prior to the drive to symbolize." And this is so, primarily because symbols are selective and distortive whereas questioning is limitless, boundless, primordially untamed! Symbols, like myths, order and structure the world. Questions explore the chaos and maybe discover the new.

The challenge to live is an existential problem. How to live is an ethical challenge. "The fact that values are relative to one's culture, time, person and purpose," argues Novak, "does not **oblige** us to be ethically indifferent...(p. 52)." Therefore, says he, the second great question before modern man in addition to "how to live?" is: **"Granted that values are relative, how do I wish to live?"** Confusion over ethics comes with the experience of nothingness, "if one has been nourished by the myth of tradition, the rationalistic myth, or the humanistic myth." Each of these myths in turn succumb to the tyranny of de-mythologization of the culture, for neither the wise men of tradition, the rational foundations of ethics in rationalism, nor the humanistic beliefs in the unique and valuable self can withstand the cold hands of nothingness which seek out the last vestiges of the old culture myth.

Where does the prospect for an ethic within the void lie? It must be found in the human arena of heightened question-asking and consciousness expansion. The discovery of the ethics of the horizon brings with it the realization that to choose life responsibly is to choose life for me and all men. The choice is free, and must be made in honesty, for to deny freedom and deride honesty is to dwell forever in the negative regions of the experience of nothingness. But to choose freely and honestly is to move out again upon the thoroughfare of myth-making and culture-creating. "To choose with less consciousness than we might is to allow our choices to be made more by others and by events than by ourselves." But, for those who would make this great ethical leap from recognizing the fact of choice to conferring value upon choices, it is, indeed, "an act of freedom, creative act, whose starting place is the experience of nothingness (p. 56)."

In addition to the values of freedom and honesty discovered in the encounter with nothingness, there are two more values, viz., courage and community. Courage is the only viable answer to the question: **"Granted that I am empty, alone, without guides, direction, will, or obligations, how shall I live?"** "In the nothingness," explains Novak, "one has at last an opportunity to shape one's own identity, to create oneself." And, in a statement suggestive of Paul Tillich's notable work entitled, "THE COURAGE TO BE, Novak encouragingly suggests, "the courage to accept despair becomes the courage to be."

The fourth value within the void is community, a threat to Marxism, Western religion, and secular liberalism alike. The experience of nothingness "desacralizes the **status quo**," it "liberates persons from conventional institutional demands," and by "collapsing distinctions," it sets the stage for creative human interaction based on freedom, honesty, and courage.

As men become increasingly responsible with their freedom, honesty, courage and sense of community, they must likewise become creatively engaged in the constructing of a new myth, myth demanding action, a myth that is captivatingly dynamic. This new myth must arise out of the midst of the void, from within the experience of nothingness. "A man's horizon," explains Novak, "is always on the move; it changes with action. Myths tell stories precisely because the essence of a story is action, and action defines the future -- A myth, therefore, is dynamic (p. 83)." And just as culture must create for itself a dynamic myth upon which to draw its life and vitality, so likewise, must the individual.

Just as there is no ideal culture which all historical cultures are destined to approximate, so neither is there an ideal self to which we
all must conform. We each must create our own myth -- to answer
the questions, Who am I? What do I wish to be? I must tell a story,
that is, create a myth by which to live. "The self-image through
which we act is, of course," says Novak, "a myth. It is the story we
tell ourselves about ourselves (p. 87)." Since story is myth and myth
demands action, the myth one creates for himself makes all the difference in the way the questions of life are answered. Novak confesses
to his myth, and to a desire to share it -- it's only a myth and, therefore, there is no external pressure to adopt it. His myth has four
characteristics: It is a "myth of raising questions;" it is a myth "that
encourages its own constant revision;" it is a "myth of self-liberation
and self-appropriation;" and it is a myth that is "radical rather than
liberal, revolutionary rather than reformist, unafraid of violence
but chastened by the self-defeating consequences of violent revolu-
tions...(p. 88)." If you like it, you can adopt it, but, if not, you must
create your own. There is no life without action; no action without
myth.

Novak closes his book with a final address to the question, What,
then, is the new myth? The first message of the new myth or new
consciousness is that "the darkness is habitable." "Those who accept
the darkness as their lot are instantly secure...through the perception
that insecurity is man's natural state...(p. 116)." Also, the new myth
requires a continual return to "inner solitude" which testifies to the
"emptiness at the heart of consciousness." Furthermore, says Novak,
the experience of nothingness which gives forth the new myth "arms
man against his own puritanism, his desire to be perfect, and his despair
at not being able to be honest, courageous, free, and brotherly." Man
must not take himself too seriously, grieve too long over his fate,
bemoan too loudly his depravity, for "a man," says Novak, "is too
insignificant to be preoccupied with his own failures (p. 117)."

Novak's answer to the search for meaning of modern man is as follows:

> What, then, is the new myth? The new sense of reality has as
> its ground the experience of nothingness. That is to say, it recog-
> nizes the emptiness, terror, and formlessness at the center of
> human consciousness. It also recognizes that a man glimpses
> the emptiness, terror, formlessness, only by virtue of his honesty
> and courage. In the exercise of his freedom, he is indebted to
> the accumulated insights of his community... The sense of rever-
> ence that disappears when totems and taboos perish is regained
> when honesty, courage, freedom, and community are cherished
> (p. 115).

BIBLIOGRAPHICAL NOTE

Michael Novak (1933-   )

There is no biographical or autobiographical sources of any significant detail on Novak's life; the student will simply need to refer to CONTEMPORARY AUTHORS, volume II for a brief sketch. Neither is there any secondary sources, since Novak's work is of very recent vintage. Nevertheless, there are a host of primary sources on a wide range of subjects, none, needless to say, of more significance for our work than his, THE EXPERIENCE OF NOTHINGNESS (N.Y.: Harper and Row, 1970). His first book was, THE OPEN CHURCH, VATICAN II, ACT II (N.Y.: Macmillan, 1964), which was a rather light-hearted if not light-headed treatment of contemporary religious moods, followed by AMERICAN PHILOSOPHY AND THE FUTURE: ESSAYS FOR A NEW GENERATION (N.Y.: Scribners, 1968). This collection of essays consists of a critique of the whole spectrum of American social institutions, and points out the difficulties Americans are having and will continue to have as we move into the 21st century. The following year, Novak follows through the implications of the AMERICAN PHILOSOPHY book with an attempt at political theorizing, entitled, A THEOLOGY FOR RADICAL POLITICS (N.Y.: Herder and Herder, 1969).

The book we have used to get at Novak's concept of meaning was written in 1970, entitled, THE EXPERIENCE OF NOTHINGNESS, and is often considered one of the most important studies of social and cultural experience of **anomie** since WWII. That same year, Novak tried his hand at fiction writing, addressing the problems of meaning and the experience of nothingness, with NAKED I LEAVE: A NOVEL (N.Y.: Macmillan, 1970). In 1971, he turned his attention to the academic study of religion, writing a college-level textbook, entitled, ASCENT OF THE MOUNTAIN, FLIGHT OF THE DOVE: AN INVITATION TO RELIGIOUS STUDIES (N.Y.: Harper and Row, 1971). This work has gained for him some respect for his scholarly abilities from the heretofore skeptical academic community.

The same year, Novak published his first study of religion and ethnicity, being a study of the decline of the American Catholic ethos, entitled, ALL THE CATHOLIC PEOPLE: WHERE DID ALL THE SPIRIT GO? (N.Y.: Herder and Herder, 1971). He followed this somewhat successful and most definitely controversial book with THE RISE OF THE UN-MELTABLE ETHNICS: POLITICS AND CULTURE IN THE SEVENTIES (N.Y.: Macmillan, 1972). This latter provocative study shows the demise of the oldtime American Dream of the melting pot, demonstrating a new sense of ethnic pride in political action and culture change. A BOOK OF ELEMENTS: REFLECTIONS ON MIDDLE-CLASS DAYS (N.Y.: Herder and Herder, 1972), was a follow-through exploring those central ingredients in the middle-classification process in American society, their present state of health, and a prognosis for the future. This is not an exhaustive list of his books, and he continues to write. Though there is currently no single study of Novak's thought, we can expect such a study to be forthcoming as his thought continues to affect the intellectual and religious communities in American Society.

CHAPTER FOUR

"Beyond Separation"

"...the prevalent sensation of oneself as a separate
ego enclosed in a bag of skin is a hallucination..."

--Alan Watts (1915-1973)

Introduction

Weary of this ego-oriented, individualistic search for life's meaning,
Alan W. Watts cries out for a shift in human consciousness away from
the myth of the "separate ego" and towards the reality that beyond
separateness lies an eternally enduring underneathness of the One.
Watts, a prolific writer particularly enamored with the ancient Hindu
philosophy of Vedanta, has summarized his investigations into the
nature of the self in, THE BOOK: THE TABOO AGAINST KNOWING
WHO YOU ARE, which essentially is addressed to the problem of
meaning by way of the fundamental question of modern man, "Who
am I?", considered in this chapter.* Watts suggests that we moderns
are in urgent need of a sense of our own existence away from the
present pervasive "hallucination...that the prevalent sensation of
oneself (is that of) a separate ego enclosed in a bag of skin... which
accords neither with Eastern science nor with the experimental philoso-
phies of the East..." The secret behind the modern taboo against
knowing who you are is that "you are the ultimate ground of being
-- your're it," and that feelings of loneliness and isolation are the
unfortunate result of the Western "illusion of the ego." The hoax
of the separate "I", the divided body and soul, is overcome, counsels
Watts, by "getting rid of the ego," ceasing from all "quest for meaning."
In the words of a Chinese philosophical work, Watts' position is summarized: "When purpose has been used to achieve purposelessness, the

---

*Unless otherwise noted, all quotations are from Watts' THE BOOK
(1970).

thing has been grasped." To facilitate this discovery is Watts' mission to modern man in Western culture.

§ § §

Alan Watts is one of those rare thinkers who comes along once in a generation or so who combines a cryptic perception of the weaknesses and foibles of his culture with a warm and passionate desire to share his personal findings and to suggest another way, beyond materialism, beyond egoism, beyond nationalism. A leading figure in what is called the consciousness-expansion movement, Watts is both a serious student of the Hindu philosophy of Vedanta and a psychosocial analyst of American culture. In THE BOOK, Watts attacks the Western problem of alienation, calling it a hoax and a culture-trick to keep people from finding out who they really are, as suggested in the subtitle, THE TABOO AGAINST KNOWING WHO YOU ARE. Though schooled in Vedantist thought, Watts is fully an experiencer in American society. His experiential affinity with Western culture is coupled with a grasp of the Eastern mysteries. Watts is uniquely gifted for the task of laying out specific guidelines for a new experience of life, not based on ego-hood, but upon the liberating realization that beyond egoism and alienation, beyond individualism and separateness, is an Eternal Oneness.

Watts has authored a score of books, ranging from ZEN and THE MEANING OF HAPPINESS to PSYCHOTHERAPY EAST AND WEST and THE JOYOUS COSMOLOGY. However, none of his books state more succinctly his thesis about the unity of man and the world than does THE BOOK. Few thinkers in this generation have had as much impact upon as diverse a reading audience as has Alan Watts. Respected as a scholar in the academy, revered as a spiritual leader in the street, Alan Watts has spoken about life -- its unity, its vitality, its universality -- and men have listened.

Alienation, says Watts, is a "big lie and hallucination," and the mission of his life as he perceived it was to liberate people from the shackles of egoism and to lead them beyond alienation to wholeness, beyond separateness to oneness. To the extent that these secrets, these mysteries, these tales of the gods can be spoken and written about, Watts does it. Watts is continually reminding the reader that Divine Mysteries and Holy Secrets are necessarily metalinguistic, i.e., beyond the capacity of human speech to communicate. Saint Paul has said: "But as it is written, eye hath not seen, nor ear heard, neither have entered into the heart of man, the things which God hath prepared for those that love him." Nevertheless, men can forever strive to communicate the incommunicable, to express the inexpressible, and by so doing, both demonstrate the inexhaustible riches of Divine Mysteries and witness to the blessings of seeking and finding them.

Watts is wont to liberate his audience from the trap of egoism, from the hallucination long propagated by society that the individual is alone, is essentially alienated from the outside world, from other individuals, and even from himself. Watts, especially concerned with society's youth, wants to share a new vision, another perspective, a different testimony about the individual's relational nature. But, as in every culture, there are always taboos, and the taboo against knowing who you are is the greatest one of all.

There needs to be a book, something akin to the "pillow book" of old Japan which illustrated love-making to a newly-wedded couple and was given them by their parents on their wedding night. A book which would put people "in the know." Watts is not optimistic about the standard-brand religions offering such knowledge about life and exposing the great taboo about selfhood, for, he thinks, the great historical religions, whether Jewish, Christian, Muslim, Hindu, or Buddist, are "like exhausted mines: very hard to dig (p. 2)."

The need for such a book is great, says Watts, "for there is a growing apprehension that existence is a rat-race in a trap," and no meaning is to be found anywhere. As man has become increasingly egocentric in his personal and cultural life, he has steadily lost the capacity to entertain belief in mystery, secret, and wonder. As man has increasingly become the alienated center of a hostile world, he has gradually lost the capacity to speak of meaning in the context of "life and love, pain and death..." and has finally reached a low-level of confidence wherein he questions "whether existence has meaning in **any** sense of the word." This washed-out state of affairs is reinforced by a supposedly logical philosophy, as for example found in Ludwig Wittgenstein, which "has tried to suppress this question" (of life's meaning) by saying that it has no meaning and ought not to be asked. And though this kind of philosophy understands its task to be to "cure people of such nonsense," nevertheless, argues Watts, "wonder is not a disease. Wonder, and its expression in poetry, and the arts, are among the most important things which seem to distinguish men from other animals..."

That Western culture has systematically denied itself self-knowledge is all too clear. The West has been outward and upward bound, conquering a hostile environment with axe and dozer, with derrick and fence. Progress-Advancement-Development have become the symbolic expressions of American culture. Granted the achievements in the world of technology, business, and medicine, what has been the price to the human community? What wounds have been dealt to human experience? Has wonder and mystery gone forever? Has the world been reduced to nothing more than a market place for the exchange of assorted goods and services? Is man able again to grasp the nature of his earthly origins? Has man not, indeed, created an environment within which he himself has become an alien? "Beyond all these is the possibility that civilization may be a huge technological success, but through methods that most people will find baffling, frightening, and disorienting -- because, for one reason alone, the methods will keep changing (p. 5)."

To approach the problem from the point of view of how can the individual get back into touch with his own feeling? or how can we re-discover our own uniqueness? is to approach the problem wrongly. The problem is even more basic, says Watts, for "the root of the matter is the way in which we feel and conceive ourselves as human beings...of individual existence and identity." Before we can speak of the pitfalls to the human community lurking in a technology gone berserk, we must first realize that "we suffer from a hallucination" about being a separated self out of a world which fosters such feelings as alienation, loneliness, and temporariness. This legacy of ego-hood is passed from generation to generation of people who unquestioningly presume that a perception (technologically and scientifically nurtured) of the world as a place of things variously labeled existing in continual separateness, including people, is a true perception of the world. Thus, people naively speak of having "come into" the world instead of having "come **out** of it, as leaves from a tree."

The resulting worldview from such experiences is, indeed, oppressive. For example, Americans have come to an attitude towards the world as essentially a "hostile" place, and thus, our greatest symbols of advancement and progress have become the bulldozer and the rocket, i.e., "the instrument that batters the hills into flat tracts for little boxes made of ticky-tacky and the great phallic projectile that blasts the sky (p. 7)." Another result of such a mechanistic worldview is that the human species is understood to be alone in the solitude of his own intelligence. There is no discourse with the world, nor is there any **common** sense among competing groups of individuals. Issues are resolved, therefore, on the basis of power-plays and gamemanship, intimidation and propaganda. There is no sense of earth which could inform the conflicting opinions of competing interest groups.

And for those who, out of the midst of this insanity of confusion and debauchery of science and technology, call for a new religion or new philosophy, Watts is not inclined to be supportive. To count on religion to save us is to display ignorance of religious history. "Religions are divisive and quarrelsome...They are a form of oneupmanship...separating the saved from the damned." Furthermore, even when a religion has settled upon doctrines, symbols, and rites that bespeak an experiential vitality, they soon "harden into institutions that must command loyalty..." Religions rely upon converts, and so contribute to propagating the big lie of ego-separateness from others and the world. "Irrevocable commitment to any religion is not only intellectual suicide," argues Watts, "it is positive unfaith because it closes the mind to any new vision of the world (p. 8)." Who can believe in a God of love concerned about man who would at the same time destroy man's mind by restricting thoughts to a single book of written words? "Books are not life," Watts points out, and "to idolize scriptures is like eating paper currency."

Though these various suggestions mentioned above as to how to cope with a growing alienation of the individual from the world are given in sincerity, Watts believes them to be misguided and wrongly conceived. "We do not need a new religion or a new bible," counsels Watts. "We need a new experience -- a new feeling of what it is to be 'I'." The problem we are presently in the midst of in our society is a false conception of the self. The notion that we are in some way a truly separate self is a hoax, and to come to understand one's total relatedness to and immersion in the world is not only taboo, but dangerously problematical to society at large. "The most strongly enforced of all known taboos is the taboo against knowing who or what you really are behind the masks of your apparently separate, independent and isolated ego (p. 9)."

Within a society which so highly values individual achievement, independence, and self-reliance, and whose laws, social institutions, and even modes of thought support such values, "it seems impossible and even absurd," says Watts, "to realize that myself does not reside in the drop alone (my selfhood is not something superficial in the scheme of the universe), but in the whole surge of energy which ranges from the galaxies to the nuclear field in my body." Conceptual thought cannot grasp it, nor would society allow knowing such a taboo even if rational discourse could reveal it.

This great taboo, this mighty mystery, the phenomenal secret so well kept within the double-walls of culture is labelled mysteriously as "the Ultimate Ground of Being" or "the Self of the World," or even "The Over-Soul." To go beyond such grandiose labels is, according to society, toying with insanity, flirting irresponsibly with the blackest of blasphemies, cavorting with the wildest of delusions. And what could elicit such cautious and threatening damnations? "The secret which my story slips over to the child," says Watts, regarding the technique of childhood storytelling as an intentional subversion of culture's well-kept secret, "is that the Ultimate Ground of Being is **you**...This, then, is the taboo of taboos: you're IT? (p. 15)." And though this may be superficially called the ultimate in megalomania -- "an inflation of the ego to complete absurdity" -- nevertheless, it is an unveiling of the great secret to which Vedanta philosophy has led Watts, viz., that nothing exists except God of whom I am only a momentary sigh.

Whereas the teaching of Vedanta as found in the sacred writings of Hinduism called the **Upanishads** reveals a God "underneath" all things, the West has too long been dominated by a God "above" everything whom we think of "as the King of the Universe, the Absolute Techno-crat who personally and consciously controls every detail of his cosmos..." This kind of Super-Grand Father projected into the sky was brought down fortunately by a combination of Copernican astrono-my, Darwinian biology, and Freudian psychology. Watts, in a Vedanta-type story of God, explains that God plays hide-and-seek with himself, and though he occasionally forgets where he is, he nevertheless always is All, the Single One. (In the words of classical Christian mysticism, which interestingly enough Watts neither quotes nor refers to, "God is the Eternal Seeker and Finder of Himself."). Thus, explains Watts, the "universe of seemingly separate things is...real only for a while, not eternally real, for it comes and goes as the self hides and seeks itself."

Among others, there is one particular caution which Watts registers early with the reader, viz., not to confuse the idea mentioned above of the self-at-one-with-God with the shallow Western notion of "unself-ishness" which is in reality a form of highly developed egoism, some-thing akin to the "we're-more-tolerant-than-you-are" variety of ego game-playing. Genuine love, says Watts, set over against such shallow notions as unselfishness and disinterested concern which lurk amidst the tangles of Western pietism, "comes from knowledge, not from a sense of duty or guilt." Neither duty nor guilt can get one beyond the sensation of ego-hood separated from an alien world. But once the breakthrough occurs, the ethical implications are startling. For upon seeing through "the illusion of the ego," explains Watts, "it is impossible to think of oneself as better than, or superior to, others for having done so (p. 19). Using the analogy of the nonevaluative relationship of egg to bird, i.e., neither can claim superiority for they are mutually related and dependent, the "egg is ego" and the "bird is the liberated self." Not the single separated part of the world with the self which encompasses all -- this is the enduring truth beyond separateness.

This feeling of self-liberation or ego-death is historically absent, with notable exceptions found especially among the heretical mystics of Christianity, from Western culture. And the "mainstay of the ego-illusion" consists of "two ignored factors," explains Watts. "The first," he continues, "is not realizing that so-called opposites, such as light and dark, sound and silence, solid and space, on and off, inside and outside, apppearing and disappearing, cause and effect, are poles or aspects of the same thing (p. 30)." And because our language, culture, and personality are devoid of such an expression of or concept for this coincidence of opposites, we perpetually deceive ourselves with vague, nebulous, and even blatantly misleading static terms like Existence, Being, God, and Ultimate Ground of Being.

Furthermore, the second factor in this ego-illusion "is that we are so absorbed in conscious attention, so convinced that this narrow kind of perception is not only the real way of seeing the world, but also the very basic sensation of oneself as a conscious being, that we are fully hypnotized by its disjointed vision of the universe." The very real fact that today American society is so obsessed with "getting it all together" or the finding of "the Real Thing" is demonstration enough that we have failed to do just that! In our society where a computer corporation uses a self-descriptive caption, "Not just truth, but Reality," and an auto manufacturing company claims their product "saves and sets you free," the symptoms of sickness from loss of a sense of meaning, purpose, direction, and relatedness to the world are clearly displayed.

Amidst it all is the struggle to make **yes** win over **no**, to make **up** win over **down**, to make **on** win over **off**, what Watts calls the game of Black-versus-White, or vice versa. "The principal form of this fight is Life-versus-Death, the so-called battle for survival, which is supposed to be the real, serious task of all living creatures." And nowhere is mankind more obsessed with survival (to the point of overkill -- such irony!) than in the West, where death becomes the great bogy, once thought of in the context of a Last Judgment but more commonly of late as "the fear that death will take us into everlasting nothingness..." Indeed, the theme of the West is sounded in the words of the Great Welsh Poet: "Do not go gentle into that good night/rage, rage against the dying of the light."

Though, admittedly, death is a great event, it must not be considered in some ghoulish way as abnormal, for it "is not a sickness at all," consoles Watts. On the contrary, "It is the natural and necessary end of human life -- as natural as leaves falling in the autumn (p. 33)." Since man has arisen from the earth as leaves sprouting on a tree in springtime, so likewise man must return as leaves to the ground in autumn. A joyous occasion should accompany such an event, since the individual is finally and completely released from his ego-prison. He awakens to the true self within, through, and underneath all supposedly separate and pitifully lonely selves.

Unfortunately, the words of the poet, "lay me down with a will," too seldom characterize the modern death-scene. "As customs now prevail," bemoans Watts, "doctors, nurses, and relatives come around with smiling masks, assuring the patient that he will soon get over it, and that next week or next month he will be back home or taking a vacation by the sea." The sooner one is willing to give up the illusion of separateness, i.e., the great ego-illusion, the sooner he will experience the true liberation of selflessness. Death brings with it the discovery that since "I" and the "other" are one and not many, "I" don't really die because "I" was never really born. Watts says, "You had just forgotten who you are" for a moment. Thus, this event is called "the great awakening of death."

There are currently two extremes regarding the nature of the individual. Both, according to Watts, are equally debilitating to the true nature of man. On the one hand, there is the Western notion of the near **sacred individual**, "the unique personal ego, separate from both nature and God" in a society which "commands him to be free and commands him to conform" in the same breath. At the other extreme, there is the **coolie**, "the cog in the industrial-collectivist machine..." The former notion we have treated, the latter Watts captures in a true story:

> During World War II a friend of mine used to fly Chinese laborers over the Hump to work on the south end of the Burma Road. The long flight was, of course, ideal for gambling, but since there was not enough cash between them to make the game interesting, the stakes were that the final loser should jump off the plane. No parachute. (p. 71)

There it is -- two equally debilitating images of man, that of an isolated person and that of an humanoid working-machine. There is a third possibility suggests Watts, hardly harnessing his passions. Man "may be seen, instead, as one particular focal point at which the whole universe expresses itself -- as an incarnation of the self, of the Godhead, or whatever one may choose to call IT." Man is neither alone nor a machine, he is rather a momentary instancing of a unique expression of God. The death of an individual, therefore, is not a disjoining but rather a withdrawing of this momentary instancing of God, the Eternal Seeker and Finder of Himself. Man is that primary agency through which God seeks and is the primary medium within whom God finds.

After the individual has discovered the great taboo, the responsible attitude is not that of **withdrawal** from the world of mirages and illusions, nor that of **stewardship** based upon a promised **future** reward (heavenly, ecological, psychic, etc.), but rather the "fullest collaboration" with an harmonious world of endless process. In a chapter entitled, "The World is Your Body," Watts points to what he considers to be the "nub" of the problem of Western man, viz., he is trapped in a "self-contradictory definition of man himself as a separate and independent being **in** the world, as distinct from a special action **of** the world (p. 81)." Thus, man never fully awakens to the reality of his relatedness to the Divine, his immersion in the Self, his oneness with the All-One, but rather is restricted in his maturity by the infantile nightmare of a separated ego.

"Now you know," says Watts. We are not separate, but only differentiated moments in the Self's seeking and finding, the Divine's game of hide-and-seek. I do not exist apart from you, and we do not exist apart from IT. Let us close with an Hassidic tale and a James Broughton poem, both quoted by Watts in admiration:

> ...As a great Hassidic rabbi put it, "If I am I because you are you, and if you are you because I am I, then I am not I, and you are not you."

> This is IT
> and I am IT
> and You are IT
> and so is That
> and He is IT
> and She is IT
> and It is IT
> and That is That.

BIBLIOGRAPHICAL NOTE

Alan Wilson Watts (1915-1973)

Alan Watts published his autobiography, entitled, IN MY OWN WAY (N.Y.: Pantheon Books), in 1972, and died the following year. A captivating, engrossing story of a man who sought earnestly to perceive the truth about the meaning of life -- an autobiography not easily forgotten, nor quickly laid aside. There is no other significant study of his life -- a few scattered and rather sketchy articles is all. And, since there is no secondary source on his thought, the student will necessarily have to get acquainted with Watts by reading primary sources -- not a bad thought, after all.

Few writers have set the writing-agenda and scholarly focus of their careers in their first published work quite as decidedly as did Alan Watts. In 1938, at age 23, Watts published, THE LEGACY OF ASIA AND WESTERN MAN: A STUDY OF THE MIDDLE WAY (Chicago: The University of Chicago Press), a significantly early effort in American scholarship to grasp the importance of Eastern thought and apply it to the ailments of Western culture. He followed two years later with a sequel to his first book, entitled, THE MEANING OF HAPPINESS: THE QUEST FOR FREEDOM OF THE SPIRIT IN MODERN PSYCHOLOGY AND THE WISDOM OF THE EAST (N.Y.: Harper and Row, 1940). Here, Watts attempts the first in a long series of efforts at dialogue between Western psychology and the techniques in Eastern religion for understanding the meaning of life, and what happiness can be in such an understanding. Several years later, he wrote a more popularly oriented study of mysticism, East and West, entitled, BEHOLD THE SPIRIT: A STUDY IN THE NECESSITY OF MYSTICAL RELIGION (N.Y.: Pantheon, 1947).

Watts was a recognized scholar and interpreter to the West of Eastern religions, and early in his life he became an important figure in the Western academic community as a specialist in Zen Buddhism. He wrote a series of books on various aspects of Zen, including such titles as, ZEN BUDDHISM: A NEW OUTLINE AND INTRODUCTION

(London Buddhist Society, 1947); ZEN (Stanford: J. L. Delkin, Publ., 1948); THE WAY OF ZEN (N.Y.: Pantheon, 1957); THIS IS IT: AND OTHER ESSAYS ON ZEN AND SPIRITUAL EXPERIMENTATIONS (N.Y., 1961); and THE SPIRIT OF ZEN: A WAY OF LIFE, WORK, AND ART IN THE FAR EAST (N.Y.: Grove Press, 1969). An expression of Watt's Easternization of Western culture is seen clearly in his study of the interrelationships of man and woman in the world in a little book, entitled, NATURE, MAN AND WOMAN (N.Y.: Pantheon, 1958).

Though THE BOOK is recognized as probably his single best statement, his PSYCHOTHERAPY EAST AND WEST (N.Y.: Mentor, 1958), is indeed, a classic statement in the East-West dialogue to which he had dedicated his life. Watts made several efforts, interesting if not successful, to set up a dialogue between Eastern religious philosophy, especially Vedanta of Hinduism and Zen of Buddhism, with Christian theology, two important efforts being, THE SUPREME IDENTITY: AN ESSAY ON ORIENTAL METAPHYSICS AND THE CHRISTIAN RELIGION (N.Y.: Pantheon, 1950), and BEYOND THEOLOGY: THE ART OF GODMANSHIP (N.Y.: Pantheon, 1964).

CHAPTER FIVE

"Man Becoming"

"To animals the world is what it is; to man this
is a world in the making, and being human means
being on the way, striving, waiting, hoping."

--Rabbi Abraham J. Heschel (1907-1972)

Introduction

Few moderns have thought more deeply about the predicament of
modern man than has the late Rabbi Abraham Joshua Heschel. Though
his writing is prolific and of consistently high quality, the expanded
form of the Raymond Fred West Memorial Lectures which he delivered
at Stanford University in 1963 has been chosen for our discussion
in this chapter.* Published under the title, WHO IS MAN?, these
six lectures constitute a **tour de force** for a theistic answer to the
question of meaning. The animality of man is all too obvious, says
the Rabbi. "The perplexity begins when we attempt to make clear
what is meant by the humanity of man." And since history requires
that we not think statically, i.e., "man is," but rather organically,
i.e., "man becoming," we must realize that "the truth of a theory
about man is either creative or irrelevant, but never merely descriptive...The image of man affects the nature of man." Man cannot
prove transcendent meaning, rather, "he is a manifestation of it."
Therefore, man is in a "relationship to meaning," and the realization
of this relationship and its resulting debt comes only when man discovers anew "the preciousness of (his) own existence."

§ § §

In a world bereft by war, anxiety, materialism, and hopelessness,

---

*Unless otherwise noted, all quotations are from Heschel's WHO IS
MAN? (1968).

Rabbi Abraham Joshua Heschel speaks with an indisputable air of humble authority about the nature of man, not of man statically conceived as "is," but organically conceived as "becoming." Rabbi Heschel was an untiring proponent of a new definition of man in an age which has lost a sense of its true humanity -- and yet, says he, not a new definition at all, but rather an ancient notion of man's relatedness to the Divine. The Rabbi plunges into the turbid history of human depravity with all the enthusiasm of a seeker after truth. He does not flinch at the reality of Auschweitz and Hiroshima, nor does he cower in the face of Hitler and The Reich. The challenge for man, as the Rabbi grasps it, is to see through, not around, these actualities of human history for that image of man which can change war into peace, anxiety into tranquility, whereby materialism can be transformed into humanism, and helplessness into faith.

The freshness and clarity of Heschel's thought is in stark contrast to the subject he chooses to address -- not man's animality, but his humanity. The Rabbi would have us know of the baseness of man, but also of his glory. He would have us know the failures and niggardliness of man, but also of his successes and ingenuity. Far from being a Pollyanna, Heschel is a man willing and able to bear the infirmaties of the weak, one who knows firsthand about the oppressiveness of the wicked, the destructiveness of human debauchery. Having himself endured the atrocities of the Nazi holocaust, Heschel speaks of man in both his holiness and his depravity, of his being and his non-being. The Rabbi speaks with a sense of ultimate meaning whether addressing the depths or the heights of human nature.

In his book, WHO IS MAN?, Rabbi Heschel begins by insisting that if we are to think responsibly of man, we must do so in human terms. And since thought implies questioning, we ask question in search of knowledge, and in this specific instance, knowledge of man. But, says the Rabbi, before man is the object of questions in search of selfunderstanding, man is already a problem to himself. We must be clear, says Heschel, between approaching man in terms of a question, i.e., the product of curiosity, and in terms of a problem, i.e., which reflects an embarrassment of knowledge. "A question," explains Heschel, "is due to knowing too little...(whereas) a problem is often due to knowing too much, to a conflict between opposing claims of knowledge (p. 2). Therefore, we must keep in mind the distinction between the actual problem of man, however conceived, and the question which comes from it.

Man is in the midst of a situation, an immersion in his own perplexities about himself. And too often, man's attempt to explain his situation, in answer to a question, is taken mistakenly to be an accurate portrayal of his actual situation itself, i.e., the problem. And, as man speculates upon his situation mediated through his questioning, "the danger always exists," cautions the Rabbi, "of those moments (of speculation) becoming distorted and even lost in the process of translation from situation to conceptualization."

The problem of man, which expresses itself in "anguish, in the mental suffering of man," arises out of the experience of conflict between "existence and expectation," i.e., the tension between who man **is** and what is **expected** of him. And upon inquiring into the nature of man, the perplexity begins when he moves beyond his **animality** (which is all too vividly demonstrated and too exhaustively belabored) to his **humanity.** This inquiry is not at the low level of parlor disputes over semantics in characterizing the human species, but at a much higher level of investigation of a reality, of a situation. "Being human," explains Heschel, "is not just a phrase referring to a concept within the mind, but a situation, a set of conditions, sensibilities, or prerequisites of man's special mode of being (p. 3)."

Heschel is distraught at the profusity of supposedly scholarly studies of man which do little more than increase the "atomization of our knowledge of man." These studies, variously labelled biological, psychological, or sociological, not only deter a legitimate perception of man as a living organic whole, but furthermore propagate a ghastly falsehood that man is categorizable according to disciplinary directives. Just as the social sciences are unable to disjoin man without destroying him, neither can philosophy claim only to be describing human nature. A philosophy of man, worthy of the name, is not only a description, but even more importantly, "it is a critique...(a) disclosure of possibilities as well as exposition of actualities of human being." And because our intellectual culture is so prone to a disjointed view of man, our entire civilization suffers from a misinterpretation of man himself.

"Self-knowledge," says the Rabbi, "is part of our being." Man is under an imperative to grasp his own nature, but with a response to the imperative comes also perplexity in trying to interpret one's own being. Not only must we inquire into the nature of man, we must also realize that his nature includes "what he thinks he is." In man's quest for self-knowledge, not only must a theory speak of man's nature, it must also realize that the theory itself "shapes and affects its subject (p. 7)." In a real sense, thinking may make it so! For "what determines one's being human is the image one adopts...The image of man affects the nature of man."

In a few terse and profoundly provocative words, the Rabbi addresses the foibles and incongruities of the behavioral sciences as they vainly attempt to facilitate a modern understanding of who man is. The behavioral sciences strive for feasible and plausible analogies between man and animal behavior. However, "we must not forget," counsels the Rabbi, "that in contrast to animals man is a being who not only behaves but also reflects about how he behaves (p. 9)."

Heschel characterizes as "intellectually stifling" the notion that behavior patterns are matters of fact pure and simple. The immodest desire for exactness, i.e., "empirical intemperance," may very well be a self-defeating process by making men blind to the "fate behind the facts" of human behavior. The inclination to "reduce all of man to what is explicit, manifest, observable" grows out of the ease with which behavior patterns are observed and described with a degree of statistical precision. The grave and detrimental mistake lurking in this bit of blatant positivistic reductionism, warns Heschel, is the equation of "man's essence with his manifestations." For as pointed out earlier, "the chief problem of man is not (so much) his nature, but what he does with his nature (p. 10)."

Whatever the medium used for gathering facts, facts of personal existence are never devoid of interpretation, for interpretation presupposes self-comprehension which involves not only "value judgments, norms, and decisions," but also results from "selective attentiveness, reflecting a particular perspective." My existence as a fact is known to me only in terms of an interpretation. And, to the extent that I perceive myself as a problem, such an awareness is rooted in self-understanding operating as "critical reflection." And, explains Heschel, "displacement of complacency, questioning the self, its acts and traits, is the primary motivation of self-understanding."

As man seeks to understand himself as situation and problem, he is grasped by wonder. And since from this wondering about himself, countless questions do arise, "the choice of question determines the trend of the inquiry." That is, the question chosen for the asking already presupposes an agenda, a pattern, an origin and direction. "To know that a question is an answer in disguise," the Rabbi says, "is a minimum of wisdom." The earlier suggestion that man is conceived not just in terms of his nature but in terms of his own expectations, returns to enable us to understand that in selecting the question to ask, we are implying an answer, i.e., "I am what I seek to know, being and knowing, subject and object, are one (p. 140)."

In an age "in which it is impossible to think about the human situation without shame, anguish, and disgust," it is impossible to be content with the answers already offered to the question about man. Those answers are blown like chaff in the searing wind of man's bloody history and are as transient as the grassless sands of the windswept desert. "The sickness of our age," wails the Rabbi, "is the failure of conscience rather than the failure of nerve (p. 15)." Man is impotent in the face of injustices; he senses his moral bankruptcy in the midst of human atrocities. Contrasting the Age of Enlightenment in which the philosopher's task was the emancipation of man from the shackles of history, Heschel says that "today, our concern seems to be to protect ourselves against the abyss of the future." The issue before us is that of the "ontological connective between human being and being human," for they "are interdependent..." "Being human, I repeat," says Heschel, "is inherent as a desideratum in human being. It is not given explicitly but is interpreted by experience (p. 17)."

Surveying this definitional problem of man through history, Heschel comes away disappointed. Whether one looks to the Delphic maxim to "know thyself," of which Plato equated the essence of knowledge, or the naturalist's belief expressed by Protagoras, "Man is the measure of all things," or the **animal rationale** of scholastic philosophy, or Benjamin Franklin's **Homo faber**, or Weston La Barre's man as "no more than (a) heat-producing metabolism with warm blood...," something is surely missing. No clear thinking man would disagree that each one of these definitions speaks accurately of man, "but," asks the Rabbi in desperation, "is this the whole truth about man?"

Heschel envisions a grand scope in his definitional quest, while smaller, more cowardly minds seek shelter amidst the particles of poorly constructed reductionistic systems which crumble under scrutiny. When we establish a definition of man, we are defining ourselves. Who defines himself in terms of a single, isolated characteristic? We do not seek to understand our animality (blatant as it is) when we strive for a definition of man; rather we long for a definition of our humanity. "Man is a peculiar being," says Heschel, "trying to understand his uniqueness (p. 22)." And his uniqueness is understandable only in human terms. To propose a definition of man built upon a definition of an ape plus the faculties of reason and speech is preposterous! "It is reported," recollects the Rabbi, "that after Plato had defined man to be a two-legged animal without feathers, Diogenes plucked a cock and brought it into the Academy."

Mocking both La Mettrie's first explicit statement which characterized

man as "the human machine," and the 11th Edition of the ENCYCLO-
PEDIA BRITANNICA'S definition of man as "a seeker after the greatest
degree of comfort for the least necessary expenditure of energy,"
the Rabbi is led to ask: "Do we still recognize man here?" We can
even admit to the scientific accuracy of the pre-Nazi Germany statement which pointed out that "the human body contains a sufficient
amount of fat to make seven cakes of soap, enough iron to make
a medium-sized nail, a sufficient amount of phosphorus to equip two
thousand match-heads, enough sulphur to rid one's self of one's fleas."
But, the proof of the Rabbi's contention that a definition of man
affects man's self-image is corroborated by the actuality of the Nazi
extermination camps, viz., that of making soap of human flesh. All
of the foregoing definitions, however scientific, when pretending
to express man's essential meaning actually contribute to the "gradual
liquidation of man's self-understanding." And after the liquidation
of self-understanding comes self-extinction.

In referring to what Heschel calls "the eclipse of humanity," i.e.,
"a new Skepticism," he compares the struggles of the great minds
of the Middle Ages trying to "discover proofs for the existence of
God." with modern man's efforts at a "proof for the existence of
man (p. 26)." We have spanned the gamut from calling man "heaven's
masterpiece" to calling him "Nature's sole mistake." And so our contemporary legacy is a definition of man propagated by one of our
cultic heroes, Tennessee Williams, who calls man (quoted from R.
E. Fitch's WHAT IS THE NATURE OF MAN, 1959), "a beast...(explaining), the only difference between man and the other beasts is that
man is a beast that knows he will die...The only honest man is an
unabashed egotist...The specific ends of life are sex and money...So
the human comedy is an outrageous medley of lechery, alcoholism,
homosexuality, blasphemy, greed, brutality, hatred, obscenity (p.
27)." And so the pitiful and miserable tale is told.

Within the question, Who is Man?, there are two interrelated questions,
says Heschel. "Specifically, our theme is not only: What is a **human
being?** but also: What is **being human?** (p. 29)." Though both dimensions
of man's situation are crucial to his becoming, it is conceivable, says
the Rabbi, that man could continue to be without necessarily being
human. Therefore, though both dimensions of man's situation are
"exposed to danger," i.e., human being and being human, the latter
is more so than the former. "Every age must in its own distinctive
manner seek out ways of rescuing man's being human from chaos
and extinction (p. 29)."

The specialness of man's being is dependent upon "certain relationships without which man ceases to be human." These relationships establish man as human being, and "human being depends upon being human." To understand the specialness of man's being is to understand these central relationshhips as modes of being which are unique to man. In asking the question, What is the self?, we are inquiring into the core of these relationships wherein, throughout all the changes and transformations I am subject to in body, intellect, and psyche, nevertheless, there is an enduring continuity of my self. To seek an understanding of man's being-as-relationship is to recognize that existence is dynamic, "is anchored in **depth**." The Rabbi seeks out those modes of being which are "fundamentals of human existence," those relationships which bespeak the essential in every man's perception of essential meaning in life.

MODES OF BEING

I. Preciousness

> Beyond all agony and anxiety lies the most important ingredient of self-reflection: the preciousness of my own existence.

In the presence of man, there is the realization of something more than simply another specimen of my species, more than a particular individual with name and personal history. For in the presence of man, we are in the company of "the only entity in nature with which sanctity is associated (p. 33)." Though there are sacred objects, holy places, etc., they are made so by man, or discovered to be so through the agency of man. "Human life," says Heschel, "is the only type of being we consider intrinsically sacred, the only type of being we regard as supremely valuable." The qualitative difference with which we see persons versus things testifies to this preciousness of man. Thinking about man is not like thinking about a thing, for with the latter I "think what I know," but with the former, I "think what I am." When inspecting man from "without," I encounter man's "being-there," but from "within," "I face my own being, here-and-now." Therefore, reasons the Rabbi, though "it is possible and legitimate to ponder being in general...it is futile and impossible to ponder human being in general...(for) there is only one way of comprehending man's being-there," continues Heschel, "and that is by way of inspecting my own being (p. 34)."

Heschel is concerned that man must discover his own special **precious-**

ness and his own **personal distinctiveness**, i.e., "how to actualize, how to concretize the quiet eminence of my being," while avoiding the dangers of a pagan anthropocentrism. "When man becomes his own idol," cautions the Rabbi, "the tablets are broken." This danger, says Heschel, is the underlying cause of the "exaggerated anxiety about death," for such idolatry of man leads him to presumptuously lay claim "to go on living without dying." And yet, man must not flee the destiny of his own being, for as the Scriptures teach: "Man is obliged to say: It is for my sake that the world was created (Sanhedrin 37a)." Man must, therefore, assert himself in his own time and place for there is a task which he alone can carry out, and a task of such importance "that its fulfillment may epitomize the meaning of all humanity."

II. Uniqueness

It is the uniqueness of man that puzzles our mind.

As with all other animals, man is biologically easy to define and classify. But with man, that which characterizes him most accurately are just those features which defy classification. "Generalization," says Heschel, "by means of which theories evolve, fails in trying to understand man." And every attempt to generalize upon man's nature ends in pitiful failure. Though trite-sounding, yet true, "No two human beings are alike." Each person is in a real sense an original without duplicate. Being human is, therefore, a "novelty," not commonplace whatsoever. And the quality of being human "consists of outbursts of singularity (p. 38)." To overlook man's singularity, personal distinctiveness, and individual idiosyncrasies is to disregard that which is most genuinely human about man. Defying the behaviorists' "statistical man," Rabbi Heschel lashes out in these especially cogent words:

No man is an average man. The ordinary, typical man, the common run undistinguished either by his superiority or by his inferiority, is the homunculus of statistics. In real life there is no ordinary, undistinguished man, unless man resigns himself to be drowned in indifference and commonness. Spiritual suicide is within everybody's reach.

III. Opportunity

It may be feasible to describe what the human species is; it is beyond our power to conceive what the human species is able to be.

Whereas animal life is a straight path, the life of man, the inner life, is a maze through which and within which man seeks, discovers, creates. The life of an animal is fixed, and what he can be is determined at birth. With man, there is no fixedness nor determinedness, there is prospect, expectation, opportunity. "One thing that sets man apart from animals," observes Heschel, "is a boundless, unpredictable capacity for the development of an inner universe (p. 39)." That which is apparent in man is only the surface of that which is possible. And, since man's "unpredictable capacity for the development of an inner universe" is that which most distinguishes him on the earth, we are forbidden to characterize man simply according to what he appears to be at any given moment. "Indeed," concludes the Rabbi, "the enigma of human being is not in what he is but in what he is able to be."

IV. Nonfinality

> It is a fatal illusion to assume that to be human is a fact given with human being rather than a goal and an achievement.

Man is a completing work of God, not a completed masterpiece. To seek the definitive edition of the human species is to misconceive the nature of man's being. To seek the finality of man is to bypass his humanity, for finality and humanity, explains Heschel, "seem to be mutually exclusive." Whereas with animal life, one can legitimately speak of the final state of being and behavior, but with man neither his being nor his behavior is fixed. "To animals the world is what it is," says Heschel, "to man (however), this is a world in the making, and being human means being on the way, striving, waiting, hoping." And just because man is never really final, he is never really safe from the dangers of losing or distorting his being. "Our being human," cautions the Rabbi, "is always on trial, full of risk, precarious (p. 42)."

V. Process and Event

> Life lived as an event is a drama. Life reduced to a process becomes vegetation.

The potentiality of man's being is not limited to an established sequence of causes and effects, but rather manifests its power in man's capacity to create, to anticipate, to plan. Man does not confront his being as a sheer block of reality, an already established actuality. Man's being is "a moment that happens." Man is not merely acted upon, he is the initiator, he decides, he intends, he challenges. "The self that I am, the self that I come upon," explains Heschel, "has the ability to combine a variety of functions and intentions in order to bring about a result, the meaning or value of which transcends my own existence (p. 42)." In attempting to understand the nature of man's being human, we must continually differentiate process from event. For process follows a given path, whereas event pioneers on the frontier of possibility; process happens regularly, whereas event occurs spontaneously and without anticipation. Process takes place in the physical world, e.g., climatic changes and earthquakes, events occur in the "inner world of man's being," e.g., Beethoven's music and Shakespeare's literature. That which is human about man dwells within events, that which is animal within process. "Being human," says the Rabbi, "is not a solid structure of a string of predictable facts, but an incalculable series of moments and acts."

VI. Solitude and Solidarity

> Human solidarity is not the product of being human;
> being human is the product of human solidarity. Indeed,
> even the most personal concern, the search for meaning,
> is utterly meaningless as a pursuit of personal salvation.

Such modes of being human as "self-sufficiency, independence, the capacity to stand alone, to differ, to resist, to defy," these are all valuable to man. "There is no dignity," explains the Rabbi, "without the ability to stand alone." As with Moses at the west bank of the Red Sea, man must stand still and withdraw from the tumult if he would truly hear. Heschel calls solitude a period of "cure and recovery," a time necessary as a protest against "the incursions and the false alarms of society's hysteria (p. 44)."

But, and in spite of the need for solitude, we must understand that there is never really a time when man is completely alone. As with the pillar saints of the 3rd century in the Egyptian desert, even in my solitary seclusion, I necessarily share life with my contemporaries -- our tears, our laughter, our pain, our joy are ours together. "Genuine solitude," says Heschel, "is not discarding but distilling humanity," for a genuine quest for solitude is actually a searching for "genuine solidarity." Man is not other than "derived from, attended to, and directed to" the being of his own community. Therefore, "for man **to be**," counsels the Rabbi, "means **to be with** other human beings." As man's being is realized in relationships, so his existence is coextensive with community.

VII. Reciprocity

> "How shall I ever repay to the Lord all the bounty He has given to me?" (Psalm 116:12) is a genuine question of man. **The dignity of human existence is in the power of reciprocity.**

The growth of the individual from infancy to maturity is reflected in the gradual shift in his experience from "obtaining and **seizing**" to "**giving** and **providing**." Heschel calls "primary data" in the makeup of life. Life is a constant receiving, life itself is a gift, and even a single breath of air Heschel calls an "inhalation of grace." The reciprocity of life is discovered through maturity, whereby the "fullness of existence" is achieved "by what we offer in return," contrary to man's blind notions of personal freedom, "for every new insight we must pay a new debt." And, since knowledge is really a debt (not private property), we must work at balancing power and mercy, truth and generosity. Reciprocity is coterminous with being a person, and therefore, says Heschel, "the degree to which one is sensitive to other people's suffering, to other men's humanity, is the index of one's own humanity (p. 47)." Consequently and finally, the great tension in man's being is not between existence and essence, but rather between existence and performance. The distinguishing mark of man is that his problem is not "to be, or not to be," but rather "**how** to be and **how** not to be."

VIII. Sanctity

> Sanctity of human life is not something we know conceptually, established on the basis of premises; it is an underived insight.

The sanctity of life is not a creation of man, but is a discovery of man's relationship to God. "Life," says Heschel, "is something **I am**," and the discovery of life's sanctity comes when one ponders the "mystery of another person's life." A primordial characteristic of all men in all times and places, indeed, a truly universal given, is man's "sensitivity to the sacred..." The sacred is beyond description in terms of goodness for example. But whereas the beauty of an object is inherent in the object, the "sanctity of a sacred object transcends the object (p. 49)." Beauty is intrinsic to a thing, sanctity is imposed from above. Though in appearance, there is a distinction between the sacred and the profane, nevertheless, "Reality embraces the actually sacred and the potentially sacred." And though there are degrees of sanctity, they all share one common aspect, viz., ultimate preciousness. "To sense the sacred," says the Rabbi, "is to sense what is dear to God."

Having viewed the question, Who Is Man? from the two underlying questions of What Is Being Human? and, What Is Human Being?, we must develop our answer to the latter question in as responsible a way as we have the former, i.e., What is being human? answered by way of a close examination of eight modes of being. Now, the question of What is the meaning of human being? must be addressed by way of two underlying themes suggested in the question, i.e, first, What is being?, and second, What is the meaning of human being? "The first theme," suggests Heschel, "dawns upon us in moments of radical amazement, when all answers, words, categories are suddenly disclosed to be a veneer, and the mystery of being strikes us as problem that lurks behind many other problems (p. 50)." The confrontation with being occurs in the primoridal regions of human experience.

And yet, being is never devoid of the human -- stark being is unknown to man. And being which is known to man, i.e., human being, goes beyond the grasp of self-understanding -- to understand the self, man must look beyond the self to that which is greater than self. He must look beyond being, his being, to meaning. "Human being is never sheer being," says the Rabbi, "it is always involved in meaning." For man to speak of being is for him to speak of his own being, human being, and man's being is known to him as meaning. "The dimension of meaning," argues Heschel, "is as indigenous to his being as the dimension of space is to stars and stones." It is man's nature that his being is charged with the responsibility to actualize meaning. However, neither being nor meaning are static, and just as man is continually challenged to actualize his own being, so is he ever "coming into meaning or betraying it."

The ordering of existence results from man's unceasing effort to identify the meaning of man as person and human being. The perpetual search is to answer satisfactorily once and for all the nagging question, What is the meaning of my being? Man is not so obsessed with finding being or losing it in non-being. No! Man's obsession is with meaning. "Mental anguish," explains the Rabbi, "is occasioned more by the experience or fear of **meaningless** being, of **meaningless** events, than by the mystery of being, by the absence of being, or by the fear of non-being (p. 52)." And though the problem of being and the problem of meaning are necessarily interrelated, they are not coextensive. For the problem of being is man's concern for his own existence, his being human as human being, whereas the problem of meaning concerns "what man means in terms larger than himself, being in terms of meaning."

Man is not in search of an understanding of who he is in terms of his own immediate existence. He seeks not a knowledgeable grasp of his existential here-and-nowness. Rather, from out of the experience of his being, i.e., his existential presence, he seeks an underlying structure of meaning. And where anguish exists in the experience of being human, i.e., the existential awareness of one's own being, such anguish is demonstrative of man's ever-present "fear of finding himself locked out of the order of ultimate meaning (p. 53)." Wherever and whenever man can, he flees such fear, he seeks shelter from meaninglessness. And, says Heschel, when man comes face to face with "a world full of anguish, of the incoherence of existence," such an encounter becomes a perpetual "nightmare."

The existentialists of the Sartrean variety are wrong when they characterize as mature those individuals who accept this anguish and thus wallow in life's meaninglessness. Man has time and time again demonstrated that there is a stake involved in being human. And that stake, claims Heschel, is in "the meaning of life." For every achievement of man, for every deed done for good, for every stride made towards justice, for every stone laid in the foundation of human equality, man "raises a claim to meaning." This meaning which legitimates man's being is not a creation but a discovery, man does not make it as he does a house; he finds it as he does a treasure. This meaning is not reducible to a "material relation and grasped by the sense organs." The behavioralists labor in vain to explain it away as this or that neurotic manifestation, as do naturalists who try to account for it in terms of bio-chemical activities in the brain.

> Inbedded in the mind is a certainty that the state of existence and the state of meaning stand in a relation to each other, that life is accessible in terms of meaning. The will to meaning and the certainty of the legitimacy of our striving to ascertain it are as intrinsically human as the will to live and the certainty of being alive (p. 54).

The meaning which we are in search of is not a meaning which derives from man, a meaning generated by good will or diligent internal probings. The task of philosophy itself, when cast in the classical tradition, is understood to be "what man dares to do with his ultimate surmise of the meaning of existence (p. 55)." That meaning which will satisfy the special search, which will pacify that most primal of human urging to grasp his true meaning, must come from above man. Man's search for "**significant being**" will end only in the transcendent wherein man's ultimate relevance is discovered. With Freud, many self-claimed mature moderns are want to cast aside the search for meaning as so much infantile play, and choose rather to define man in terms of so many biological drives and psychological needs, and choose to define human happiness in terms of the satisfying of such needs and drives.

The Rabbi, on the other hand, is not accepting of such a position so quickly taken and easily kept. After satisfaction, what? asks Heschel. Happiness does not so easily pacify. Rather, says he, happiness worth the having "may be defined as the certainty of being needed," and for those who to the question, And who needs man? quickly answer "society," Heschel follows by asking, And who needs society? But this will not do! "To say that life could consist of care for others, of incessant service to the world," counsels the Rabbi, "would be a vulgar boast. What we are able to bestow upon others is usually less and rarely more than a tithe." Man cannot establish his own meaning in terms of himself and his own existential being, nor upon his society for both I individually and we collectively are in need of an ultimate meaning which transcends our own personal and temporal being.

Meaning and human being are inseparable. Man is a being in search of "significant being," i.e., of ultimate meaning of existence. But by connecting human being and ultimate meaning with the question of "And who needs man?," we are suggesting that not only is man "part of a whole...but (is) an answer to a question, the satisfaction of a need (p. 63)." By phrasing the relationship of man to meaning in this way, Heschel would have us to understand that this unceasing quest of man for the ultimate relevance of being is in "response to a requiredness of existence..." It demonstrates a discovery that man is not precious only to himself in human terms but is precious in terms of ultimate meaning. It is likewise an experiential realization that, no matter how hard he may try, "Man cannot prove transcendent meaning" because "he is a manifestation of transcendent meaning."

The nature of man's being in the context of meaning is one of relationship -- "man is a being involved in a relationship to meaning." The only context within which man can be understood is that of meaning, and since "meaning is a primary category not reducible to being as such," we must grasp man by grasping his relationship to meaning. "Man is in need of meaning," says Heschel, "but if ultimate meaning is not in need of man, and he cannot relate himself to it, the ultimate meaning is meaningless to him (p. 73)." That relationship which authenticates human being in search of meaning is a relationship of reciprocity. Heschel points to a crucial distinction between the Greek formulation of the search for meaning as "man in search of a thought," and the Hebrew formulation as "God's thought (or concern) in search of man." Biblical thought centered upon "man's being known by God" and the **"awareness of God's interest in man"** rather than "man's knowledge of God."

As man comes to know that his being has meaning as ultimate significance only in relationship to God, he comes to value life as **partnership** between himself and God. "The tragedy of modern man," explains the Rabbi, "is that he thinks alone (p. 76)." To the man of the Bible, he is given to understand that "beyond all mystery is meaning." The mistake which has produced anxiety and tragedy in modern times is man's failure to perceive the meaning beyond the mystery. Modern man flees from meaning by fleeing from mystery. "The mystery is not a synonym for the unknown," says Heschel, "but rather a term for a meaning which stands in relation to God." And the difference between finite meaning and transcendent meaning is that the former has beauty but no grandeur, it pleases but offers no redemption, is thinkable and not beyond comprehension. When man comes to know transcendent meaning, his being takes on new significance -"Humanization is articulation of meaning inherent in being (p. 96)."

When man comes to this discovery of meaning which transcends and offers itself to his own being, he senses a personal debt. "We come closer to an understanding of religion," says Heschel, "by defining one of its roots as a sense of personal indebtedness." Man becomes anxiety-ridden when he does not know what is expected of him, and when he accepts what Heschel calls the "prerequisite of sanity." Furthermore, says Heschel, "the reality of being human depends upon man's sense of indebtedness being a response to transcendent requiredness. Without such awareness man is spiritually inane, neither creative nor responsible." Acceptance of one's debt in a world he does not own is the first step in mature responsibility towards Divine-Human Reciprocity. Man stands between the earth and heaven as that concrete instancing in the here-and-now of transcendent meaning. Through man's search for ultimate meaning God finds himself.

Man is more than what he is to himself. In his reason he may be limited, in his will he may be wicked, yet he stands in a relation to God which he may betray but not sever and which constitutes the essential meaning of his life. He is the knot in which heaven and earth are interlaced (p. 103).

BIBLIOGRAPHICAL NOTE

Abraham Joshua Heschel (1907-1972)

Biographical Sources

There is no substantial biography of Heschel's life yet, and neither is there much by way of autobiographical information. Several standard sources offer the general biographical facts of his life, such sources as WHO'S WHO IN WORLD JEWRY, 1965, and CURRENT BIOGRAPHY YEARBOOK, 1970. An article about Heschel, entitled, "Militant Mystic," appeared in TIME, 101:43, January 8, 1973, and L. Finkelstein has written an interesting piece entitled, "Three Meetings with Abraham Heschel," for AMERICA, 128:203-9, March 10, 1973.

Primary Sources

Rabbi Heschel was a prolific writer, but for our purposes, there are several key books which must be mentioned. His most important early work was in religious philosophy which contributed to his international prominence during the following two decades, entitled, MAN IS NOT ALONE: A PHILOSOPHY OF RELIGION (N.Y.: Farrar, Straus, and young, 1951), being a **tour de force** for a theistic view of man. In sequel fashion, he followed four years later with a book entitled, GOD IN SEARCH OF MAN: A PHILOSOPHY OF JUDAISM (N.Y.: Farrar, Straus, and Cudahy, 1955), which was essentially a further elaboration of his 1951 book but overtly centered upon the Jewish faith and tradition.

The previous year, he had gathered a collection of his views on the devotional life, which in a real sense displays the deep religious character of Heschel's life, in a book entitled, MAN'S QUEST FOR GOD: STUDIES IN PRAYER AND SYMBOLISM (N.Y.: Scribner's, 1954). In 1962, he wrote his highly acclaimed study of the Prophets of Israel, entitled, THE PROPHETS (N.Y.: Harper and Row, 1962), followed by a collection of interpretive essays on the Jewish religion, selected, edited and introduced by F. A. Rothschild, entitled, BETWEEN GOD

AND MAN: AN INTERPRETATION OF JUDAISM (N.Y.: Free Press, 1965). A small devotional yet scholarly book, THE EARTH IS THE LORD'S AND THE SABBATH (N.Y.: Harper and Rowe, 1966), appeared a year later, but one of the best of his works has appeared posthumously, entitled, A PASSION FOR TRUTH (N.Y.: Farrar, Straus, Giroux, 1973), which in a real sense is the Rabbi at his best -- talking of life and its meaning.

Secondary Sources

There are three rather good secondary sources on Heschel's thought. The most important to date, and for the student most valuable, is a book published in the PROMISE OF THEOLOGY series by F. Sherman, entitled, THE PROMISE OF HESCHEL (Philadelphia: Lippincott, 1970). The other two sources are in a collection of essays on various recent philosophers and theologians of Judaism, the first being by Patrick Granfield, THEOLOGIANS AT WORK (1967), and the other by Eliezer Berkovits, MAJOR THEMES IN MODERN PHILOSOPHERS OF JUDAISM (N.Y.: Ktav Publishers, 1974).

CHAPTER SIX

"The Joyful Proclamation"

"...this statement that the human spirit is naturally
Christian many be valid as an obstinately
joyful proclamation."

--Karl Barth (1886-1968)

Introduction

Generally regarded as the most important Protestant thinker of modern
times, and certainly of the 20th century, Karl Barth has developed
with relentless rigor a restatement of the fundamental principles
of the Reformation called variously "neo-orthodoxy" and "crisis theology." Like Luther's commentary on Romans, Barth's commentary,
THE EPISTLE TO THE ROMANS (1918), was a bomb-blast that shook
the Christian world. Since that notable beginning, Barth has without
lull continued to call modern man's attention to God in Christ, wherein
the true meaning of man's life must be found. In this chapter, we
will consider three short essays written by Barth towards the end
of his life collected under the title, THE HUMANITY OF GOD.* In
the first essay, Barth explains the nature of his criticism of 19th
century theology which, he suggests, was "more interested in man's
relationship to God than in God's dealings with man, or...more in
the **beneficia Christi** than in Christ Himself." In the second essay,
Barth begins: "The humanity of God! Rightly understood that is
bound to mean God's relation to and turning toward man." In the
Word of God found in the Scriptures, "man recognizes himself as
being under God's judgment and grace, as the receiver of His promise
and His command...in which (man) recognizes his own God in the

---

*Unless otherwise noted, all quotations are from Barth's THE HUMAN-
ITY OF GOD (1968).

deity of Jesus Christ as well as himself in His humanity." Thus, says Barth speaking of "a world which regards itself as of age (and proves daily that it is precisely not of age) that the so-called 'outsiders' are really only 'insiders' who have not yet understood and apprehended themselves as such." Barth's concentration upon God in Christ leads him to conclude that the human spirit is naturally Christian may also be valid as an obstinately joyful proclamation." The third essay is a discussion of the "gift of freedom" in the context of "the foundation of evangelical ethics." The essay is developed in accordance with three summary propositions: 1) **God's Freedom is His very own,** 2) **Man's Freedom is his as the gift of God,** 3) **Evangelical ethics is the reflection upon the divine call to human action implied by the gift of freedom.**

§ § §

With the exceptions of possibly Martin Luther and John Calvin, no Protestant theologian has affected the life of Western Christendom with such profound challenge and superlative example as has Karl Barth. During a time, just following the first World War, when the Church came up against the devastating consequences of the shallow anthropocentric optimism of 19th century theology, Barth came to the Church's rescue with a theology called "crisis theology," or "neo-orthodoxy." Falling heir to 19th century incongruities, Barth and his students were initially forced to live with the optimistic anthro-pocentrisms of a theology which supposed that to talk of God meant little more than to talk of man with raised voice. In view of man's inhumanity to man so blatantly displayed on the battle fields of France, modern turn-of-the-20th-century man was coming to the realization that the challenge before the Christian community was not to stubborn-ly hold to hope in man's goodness, but rather to turn humbly to faith in God's grace in the face of man's wickedness.

Barth's long career, as reflected in the Bibliographical Essay at the end of this study, was dedicated to a search for the meaning of God revealed in The Word -- God in Christ. Often scathingly critical and never without polemic, Barth set about to systematically dismantle the 19th century theology built upon Schleiermacher's religion of human emotion. Neither Schleiermacher's "sense and taste of the infinite" nor Troeltsch's "religious **a priori**" could withstand Barth's attack. If we reduce the faith of Christians, i.e., belief that God has revealed himself in Jesus Christ, to simply another religion along-side world religions such as Judaism, Buddhism, Islam, and Hinduism, Christianity loses its truth, integrity, and the uniqueness of its good news. Christianity is not just another historical religion, joining the ranks of the spacio-temporal, socio-cultural relativities of man's belief systems. The truth of Christianity sets it apart from religion, for Christianity is the joyful proclamation of God's love for man manifest in Jesus Christ. Mankind is freed from the shackles of religion, for God's grace has liberated us from law and ritual; we are now given hope through God's love expressed to men in the man, Christ Jesus.

Toward the end of Barth's scholarly career, he gave three profoundly provocative and surprisingly fresh lectures, spaced over a four year period, which have proven to be Barth's most popular work among laymen and theological students. The collection, published under the title of the second lecture, THE HUMANITY OF GOD, consists of three lecture-essays. In the first essay, Barth reflects autobiographically upon his career and his destructive-constructive attitudes towards the 19th century, entitled, "Evangelical Theology in the 19th Century." Every student of theological history must wrestle with Barth's appraisal here, reflected in our opening remarks to this chapter. The second essay, "The Humanity of God," is an exploration into the relationship of man to God and God to man reflected in Christ Jesus. The third essay, "The Gift of Freedom: Foundations of Evangelical Ethics," follows out the implications for an evangelical ethic within the context of Barth's christology.

To speak of God, says Barth, is to speak of God for man. Though the nature of God is inexhaustibly transcendent, and thus men need not attempt to capture God in definition, nevertheless, when men speak of God -- and they cannot for long forego such talk -- they speak from the human perspective, their only legitimate perspective. And therefore, to the extent that man can say anything of significance about God, it is to speak of God's "existence," His "intercession," and His "activity for man." Man does not establish this Divine-Human relationship, as if man were able to draw God into dialogue at will. Rather, through the "free grace in which He wills to be and is nothing other than the God of man," God turns toward and engages man by speaking through "promise" and "command." As God is encountered in a relationship with man which Divine grace alone freely establishes, man comes to know only that of God which he is able, viz., "the humanity of God."

In contradistinction to the legacy of liberal 19th century theology established by Schleiermacher and Troeltsch which placed man and culture at the center of attention at the expense of God's Deity, Barth and supporters after the First World War reaffirmed the centrality

of God's Deity **vis a vis** man and culture.   This shift from anthropocentric to theocentric theology was necessarily polemical in order
that the Church's attention might once again, after the order of Luther
and Calvin, be drawn upon the absolutely sovereign God of Grace
and away from sinful and helpless mankind. It is God who "unveils,
announces, and reveals Himself to man." This was the theme. The
mystery of God's willing and being was spoken of as a "wholly other"
and "Holy One."

The necessary but unfortunate result of this pendulum swing from
man to God was, says Barth, that "for us (during the early years of
the 20th century), the **humanity** of God at that time moved from
the center to the periphery, from the emphasized principal clause
to the less emphasized subordinate clause (p. 38)."   The dangers
of anthropocentric religionization of the Christian faith were seen
to be so threatening to the God-centered integrity of the doctrine
of the Incarnation -- God in Christ among men -- that an unrelenting
attack upon its charming spell over the church was imperative. The
resulting relentless attack upon a theology which placed man and
culture at the center (thereby pre-empting theocentric faith) inevitably
subordinated any talk of God's humanity.

Though God's humanity was never overtly denied, Barth does admit
that he "should indeed have been somewhat embarrassed if one had
invited me to speak on the humanity of God -- say in 1920..." Times
have changed, and there has also been a change in the task and challenge of Christian theology which must unfailingly readdress its own
time and place from within the arena of faith mediated in the Word
of God. Speaking of today, Barth says: "Our problem is this: to
derive the knowledge of the humanity of God from the knowledge
of His deity (p. 28)."

Barth conceives his task in this essay to be to demonstrate how we
are to move from God's **deity** to His **humanity**. But, says Barth, before
we can grasp this crucial point, we must first understand the context
within which, and the historical background out of which, this point
has come. The fact that Barth's commentary on **Romans** (1918, 1920,
1933) was traumatizingly provocative when it first appeared -- speaking of God in bold and unequivocatingly stark reverence, and of man
as weak, sinful, and in need of Divine grace -- bespeaks the timorous
state of early 20th century theology. From 1799 (the appearance
of Schleiermacher's **SPEECHES**) to 1918 (Barth's ROMANBRIEF),
Christian thought had been dominated by a tripartite motif of a religion-
istic, anthropocentric, and humanistic character. Human piety, both

Christian and otherwise, had become the object of theological development to the exclusion of all other themes. The Christian faith was
reduced to a religion or religious culture and theological method
was conceived as history and phenomenology of religions. Not only
in ethics and doctrine was historical relativizing taking place, but
especially was it evident in dogmatics and the study of Scripture.

Within such a liberal genre, who could speak or know of God's Deity,
for hardly did theologians stop from speaking of religious man and
his culture long enough to refer even to God's humanity. "For this
theology," explains Barth, "to think about God meant to think in a
scarcely veiled fashion about man..." Man was conceived as **homo
religiosis** and Christian man was understood as the most advanced
of religious men. And therefore, Christian man and his culture became
the glory of theology! "To speak about God," continues Barth, "meant
to speak in an exalted tone...about this man...Here man was made
great at the cost of God (p. 39)." Nineteenth century theology lost
sight of its focus upon God's free will to act graciously in the world,
and became enamored with the poor pitiful recipient of Divine grace,
viz., man himself.

After a while, the Church began to founder and lose sight of its mission
and witness -- an inevitable result of valuing the **object** of grace
instead of the **source** of grace. Christian man had temporarily and
regrettably forgotten about the "divine God who is someone other
than man, who sovereignly confronts him, who immovably and un-
changeably stands over against him as the Lord, Creator, and Redeemer
(p. 49)." By so forgetting, the Christian man lost sight of that from
"whence cometh his salvation," and began to delight and boast in
his unmerited gift. But when man turns away from the royal face
of God and looks upon the beleaguered and pathetic face of man,
he, as did St. Peter walking upon the water, begins to sink in self-
helplessness. When man takes it upon himself to become the origin
and center of that which is religious, of that within which divinity
presumably springs forth, he is dangerously close to pride which comes
before the fall. But such a notion results in a pious monologue with
oneself. God is excluded.

The danger of quietism and mysticism alike is the danger of spiritual
pride wherein men become satisfied with their own weak attempts
at approximating God's grace by their own initiatives. God was in
danger of being reduced, says Barth of 19th century theology, "to
a pious notion," and "to a mystical expression and symbol of a current
alternating between a man and his own heights and depths." Lost

was the "God who is also man's free partner in a history inaugurated by Him and in a dialogue ruled by Him...(p. 40)."

Finally, and at this point when, says Barth, we "had drained the different chalices of this theology to the last drop," he and some of his colleagues could no longer side with such a notion. Time had come to dress the sails and steer a different course. There were, indeed, countless factors, great and small, which facilitated this shift and which nurtured a redress of theological method. The growing uneasiness with a faith reduced to a world-historical religion and the Christian life cast as an advanced religious expression helped bring on the crisis of theology. Also, there was a creeping suspicion that beyond "the musty shell of the Christian-religious self-consciousness" was a God wholly other who acts and speaks in history. Furthermore, the outbreak of the First World War with all its inhuman atrocities produced a disenchantment with man's goodness and a disillusionment with a definition of man as intrinsically religious and ethical. And too, the messages of Kierkegaard, Dostoyevsky, and others bursting from out of the depravity of those war years spurred the younger theologians on in their search, like Barth, for the ground of faith.

Through such gradually accumulating destruction wrought upon an old and impotent anthropocentric theology came a concomitant realization that faith and the theological method of the Church must not build upon a confidence in man's religiosity and his intrinsic morality, and definitely not upon his inner "secret divinity." Gone were such shallow foundation stones. The theology of the Church needed to rediscover the source of its strength which has always resided outside humankind and beyond himself.

"The stone wall we first ran up against," recounts Barth, "was that the theme of the Bible is the deity of God, more exactly God's deity... (p. 41)." Almost a rediscovery of God, this repristinization of theology led again to the discovery of God's transcendence, His sovereignty, His freedom in history, and mostly His relationship to man. Only through such a discovery, says Barth, "could we understand the voice of the Old and New Testaments," and only then could they feel capable of being "theologians...ministers of the divine Word." The blind alley had been escaped through a major change of direction -- "The ship was threatening to run aground," says Barth, "the moment was at hand to turn the rudder an angle of exactly 180 degrees."

The tide has now been turned. No longer can men honestly and wisely traffic in the rhetoric of 19th century theological liberalism while standing under the sanction of more mature theology. It is in God's grace, not in man's religiousness, where salvation is to be found. The joyful proclamation is not of man's discovery of himself, but of man's encounter with God. And though the need of shifting direction was necessary and rightly accomplished, Barth is now hoping to move beyond the "preponderantly critical polemic movements...;" away from such newly invented expressions as the famous "wholly other" breaking in upon us "perpendicularly from above," the God-man relationship characterized as the "infinite qualitative distinction." Almost regretfully but nevertheless honestly, Barth proclaims, "How we cleared things away!" All anthropocentrism, all religiosity, and anything that "even remotely smacked of mysticism and morality, of pietism and romanticism, or even of idealism" was scrutinized or censored, bracketed or mocked with "a derisive laugh."

And, there were those ever-present bold assurances which characterized this new shift in theology, e.g., "there is in the Bible only **one** theological interest, namely, that in God; that only **one** way appears, namely, that from above downwards; that only **one** message can be heard, namely, that of an immediate forgiveness of sins both in prospect and in retrospect (p. 43)." When the pendulum swings, it covers the gamut. From man-centered to God-centered, there was in earlier times such a bifurcated view of the matter as to preclude any talk of the humanity of God. Ethics focused upon "man's sickness unto death," while redemption implied a complete abolition of man's creatureliness. Indeed, says Barth, the result was "to stand Schleiermacher on his head," which is to say, "make **God** great for a change at the cost of **man**." All of this reshifting in theological thought and method towards a God of transcendence, sovereignty, and wholly otherness, and away from religionism, anthropocentrism, and humanism prevented the notion of the humanity of God from coming into its rightful place in Christian thought.

Understandable, indeed, was the infatuation with God's "wholly otherness" of these young theologians who had gorged themselves on humanistic religiosity only to suffer from perpetually unquenched hunger for the God of the Bible. But where did this change of direction go astray?, Barth has asked. "I believe," he confesses, "...that we were wrong exactly where we were right," viz., the discovery of this new knowledge of the **deity** of God led theologians to so overstate the case that the **humanity** of God was overshadowed. There was a danger here, to be sure, a danger of so picturing the deity of God as to devastate man in His Presence. Indeed, the God of the Bible called Yahweh-Kyrios was awful, but was nonetheless still the God of Abraham, Isaac, and Jacob. During these early days of direction-changing, says Barth, God was treated in "isolation, abstracted and absolutized" at the expense of man, "this miserable wretch." The good done by this shift, finally, was ill spoken of. The time has now come, counsels Barth, to seek that balance between God's deity and His humanity.

We must grasp the meaning of God for man within the context of the "**deity of the living** God", says Barth, and that can only be done when we realize that God's deity can find "its meaning and its power only in the context of His history and His dialogue with **man**, and thus in His **togetherness** with man (p. 45)." This togetherness is not of man's making, but rather is derived from the sovereignty, the ground and determination of God alone. And though originating with the initiative of God's own grace, nevertheless, it is a togetherness with man, for God's being and deity are not exemplified in a "vacuum as a divine being-for-Himself," says Barth. On the contrary, He manifests His existence, His power to speak and act in history "as the partner of man..." **That**," says Barth, "is a precise and authentic expression of the Living God." And, "the freedom in which he does **that** is His deity."

Such freedom to act in history -- to speak, to appear, to exist -- is an expression of the humanity of God's Deity. That is to say, "It is precisely God's **deity** which, rightly understood, includes his **humanity**." To know God's deity is in a real sense to know God's humanity. Whereas the 19th century anthropocentric theology displayed a lack of grasping God's deity because of an inflated view of man, the early 20th century theocentric theology reflected a faint capacity to perceive God's humanity due to an inordinate fixation on the "wholly otherness" of God's deity.

Mankind cannot come to know of the humanity of God's deity except in Jesus Christ. With Jesus Christ, we are confronted with God incarnate in human flesh. We are dealing neither "with **man** in the abstract" nor "with **God** in the abstract" -- Not a humanity composed of sufficient religious emotion and religious morality as to make God expendable, nor with a deity which exists wholly separate such as to make man expendable. But in Jesus Christ, God is not apart from man, nor man apart from God. "Rather," explains Barth, "in Him we encounter the history, the dialogue, in which God and man meet together and are together, the reality of the covenant **mutually** contracted, preserved, and fulfilled by them." It is in Jesus Christ that the humanity and deity of God are convergent, testifying to God's loyal partnership with man and man's with God.

To know of God's deity is to see the humanity of Christ; to know of God's humanity is to sense the deity of Jesus. Jesus Christ is neither confused nor divided between God and Man, but is both. Therefore, he stands as the only True Mediator between Man and God, the Reconciler of heaven and earth. As Mediator and Reconciler, he comes to man on God's behalf and to God on man's behalf. "Thus," Barth continues, "He attests and guarantees to man God's free **grace** and and at the same time attests and guarantees to God man's free **gratitude** (p. 47)." And in such a capacity, Jesus Christ becomes for man and for God "the **Revealer** of them both."

Since God has made the humanity of His deity known to the world through Jesus Christ, we can no longer be content to simply ask, Who and What is God? Rather, now we are led to ask the more meaningful question, Who and What is **God in Jesus Christ**? In Holy Scripture, it is the existence of Jesus Christ himself which proclaims God's deity, because it is God himself in Christ as subject who speaks with authority and acts with sovereignty. It is, truly, God in Christ that we see in Holy Scripture which portrays simultaneously humanity and deity. It is God in Christ "in whom all freedom has its ground, its meaning, its prototypes;" God in Christ is the "initiator, founder, preserver, and fulfiller of the covenant;" for God is sovereign Lord, and Creator of His own partner. To know this is to know of God's preeminent presence in Jesus Christ, and not to know is to fail to grasp either the reality of God's deity or of His humanity. "As the Son of God," says Barth, "Jesus Christ is the Son of Man."

Man has been exalted, not by any merit of his own part, but because God has condescended, for in Jesus Christ, explains Barth, "man's freedom is wholly enclosed in the freedom of God." And the nature of this "high freedom in Jesus Christ," says Barth, "is His **freedom for Love** (p. 48)." The bending downward of God expresses His love for man while the turning upward of man expresses man's gratitude to God. The sequence is irreversible yet demonstrative of the togetherness of man and God, best seen in Jesus Christ who embodies "the highest communion of God with man." The mystery of the Incarnation is in God's freedom to exist in and for Himself yet choosing to be with and for man, while not "in the slightest forfeiting His deity!" In Jesus Christ, men confront the sovereignty of God's deity and the compassion of His humanity. Only in Jesus Christ can man know of this mystery -- the humanity of God's deity. God's communion with Man bespeaks this Living Mystery.

It is the deity of God which **"encloses humanity in itself,"** for in Jesus

Christ, it is established once and for all eternity "that God does not exist without man." The mystery of God's concern for man is compounded when we ponder His freedom. "What is man," asked the Psalmist, "that Thou art mindful of him?" Though God could exist alone unto Himself without either man or world, He has nevertheless chosen man! For man to choose man is pathetic, but for God to choose man is Divine Mystery. And, says Barth, it is this "mystery...which meets us in the existence of Jesus Christ." Out of freedom, not need, God chooses to be **for** man and to be **with** man. He loves man and seeks to be his partner.

"In this divinely free volition and election, in this concern for him, His free substitution for him -- this is God's humanity." In Christ, God shows His concern, His love, His compassion for man. And, since in the words of Martin Luther, Christ is "the mirror of the fatherly heart of God," Nietzsche's desire to characterize man as something to be overcome is an impudent lie," says Barth.

After having discovered the Christological center of Christian theology, we must now explore the far-reaching consequences of such a discovery. Barth lists five such consequences. First, this discovery of God's humanity results in a rather explicit **distinction of man.** This distinction is due man solely because God has freely chosen him and has willed to exalt him as his partner. And, since "God is human in this sense," this distinction is actually **due** man, nevertheless. And therefore, we are compelled to think of "**every human being**...as one to whom Jesus Christ is Brother and God is Father..." For those who do not know this good news, those of us who do are obliged to tell them and for those who already know it, we are responsible in strengthening them in their knowledge. Otherwise, our silence is a **de facto** renunciation of Christ as Brother and God as Father.

This distinction due man by virtue of God's humanity is a free gift of God's deity, and therefore, is not subject to being lost because of man's wickedness and sinfulness, nor can its goodness be diminished. "Man is not elected to intercourse with God," Barth cautions, "because, by virtue of his humanity, he deserved such preference. He is elected through God's grace alone (p. 53)." To forget this is to fall into the dangerous anthropocentrism of the 19th century. And though we cannot meet God in all of his sovereignty and being, we can meet Him within the boundaries of His humanity. Though His nature is inexhaustible and His being inconceivable, man can by virtue of God's grace meet Him. "He does not reject the human!" exclaims Barth. Each man, in his own time and place, must meet God. And though human culture bespeaks man's depravity and his perpetual incapacity to do good by himself, nevertheless, to the extent that culture is "the attempt of man to be man," he is striving to hold on to the gift of his humanity, thus glorifying God.

A second consequence of our discovery is that of a definite theme given to **theological** culture. "Since God in His deity is human," explains Barth, "this culture must occupy itself neither with God in Himself nor with man in himself but with the man-encountering God and the God-encountering man and with their dialogue and history, in which their communion takes place and comes to its fulfillment (p. 55)." If, as stated earlier, culture is man's attempt to be himself by means of holding the "good gift of his humanity in honor," the theological culture is the actualization of this attempt by centering upon the Divine-Human Encounter.

For the Christian, theological culture is as real as anything in the phenomenal world. Whereas secular culture fails to realize its aspirations for human self-actualization, theological culture succeeds because of the recognition of that beyond man which makes man possible. The Divine-Human dialogue, i.e., the God-man communion, occurs only by means of Jesus Christ. Theology cannot introduce Jesus Christ and neither can culture introduce God. Furthermore, neither theology nor culture can bring about "dialogue, history, and communion" within the God-man encounter. This encounter is solely dependent upon the Holy Scriptures. Theology, and therefore theological culture, is able to "think and speak" only to the extent that they look singularly upon Jesus Christ. Theology is dependent upon Holy Scriptures "according to which," says Barth, "the covenant is **in full effect** and in which Jesus Christ **witnesses to Himself.**" Theology hears this witness, "trusts it and is satisfied with it."

The problems of 19th century theology grew out of a loss of this objectivity in the theme of theology. Theology has always been given its subject matter as God in Christ revealed in Scripture, but the 19th century represented a movement away from its true subject and towards man. Man is the subject of theology only in the context of the Divine-Human encounter revealed in Jesus Christ. On this point, Barth is adamant: "Theology must hold fast to this objectivity in its exegesis: in its investigation, presentation, and interpretation of the Christian past and present; in its dogmatics and ethics; and in its preaching, instruction, and pastoral ministry (p. 55)." Theology must keep vigilance lest it be drawn astray from this task.

From within this context of objectivity, theology must continually be elucidating the encounter of God with man and subsequently of man with God. That is, theology deals both with the "act and word" of God's grace and with the "act and word" of man's gratitude. When theology stays with this dual task, it will manifest by its very method and application the humanity of God's deity, and can legitimately be characterized as, in Barth's words, "cultivated theology." By doing this, theology takes unto itself the existentialists' claim that man cannot speak of God without speaking of man, without taking to itself the "old error," says Barth, "that one can speak of man without first, and very concretely, having spoken of the living God."

Given the Christian community's discovery of God's humanity revealed in Jesus Christ, a third consequence of this knowledge calls for "a definite **attitude** and **alignment** of Christian theological thinking and speaking (p. 57)." The concrete manifestation of God as man in the world precludes theology from functioning as an abstract theory or in a vacuous metaphysic. Theology is not a monologue, discoursing in abstract truths about God and man, verifying, reflecting, and reporting to itself. Theology grows out of and is reflective of the dialogics of the Divine-Human encounter. God, epitomized in the God-Man, constitutes the **genre** for theologizing, and the Holy Scriptures establish the context. No longer can men speculate about the nature and meaning of God in the metaphysical rubrics of philosophy, for in Jesus Christ revealed in Holy Scripture, God has manifested His Humanity and set the stage for encounter, dialogue, discourse, and intercourse with man.

In view of its objects, "the fundamental form of theology," says Barth, "is the prayer and the sermon." And this is so because, as prayer to God and address to man, they are the supreme expressions of the dialogics of the Divine-Human encounter. In prayer, as in the sermon, the most personal affairs of all men as individuals are treated -- the "commerce between God and man is personalized in Jesus Christ. And only in knowing Jesus Christ can men come to this personal commerce with God, the discovery of God's humanity within His deity. Nevertheless, theology not only presupposes that the dialogics of the Divine-Human encounter is personalized for **all men** and **each man** in Jesus Christ, but theology also "presupposes that there are many -- many too many -- who **do not yet** or **no longer** or **do not rightly** know (indeed, in some way all this applies to every man) that it is necessary and imperative to proclaim all men, to call them together, and to communciate (p. 57)." This, says Barth, is the central concern of Christian speaking -- discourse which focuses upon God's Word of reconciliation and man who hears the Word and must respond.

The Word, revealed in Christ through Holy Scripture, is the message which man hears, which invites and summons him to respond. Man's response is not to theory and speculation, not to philosophy and metaphysics, but to "faith and obedience," away from the "mere 'interest' of the spectator" to that of "genuine participation." This engagement, this total enrapturing of the hearer occurs when man "recognizes his own God in the deity of Jesus Christ as well as himself in His humanity." Theology is the outcome, not the instigator, of this engagement -- God alone initiates, invites, beckons through His Word, the **Kerygma.** And the Word, the kerygma, is for all men, for those who do hear and for those who do not, for those who can and those who cannot. The Christian community, therefore, comes to understand that there are never any **real** "outsiders" as there are never any **real** "insiders." The difference among men is between those who have heard and those who have not heard, between those who have come to know of this total engagement with God's humanity in Jesus Christ because of God's grace to all men and those who have not understood or responded.

Therefore, counsels Barth, there must never evolve a distinguishing language for insiders and outsiders -- the message of the Word "is a strange piece of news in any case," and thus the theologian's task is to communicate the "good news" in understandable terms while maintaining an integrity of experience communicable through traditional language. If this "great piece of news, i.e., the message of the eternal love of God" for man revealed in Jesus Christ, is shared simply and unpretentiously (either in scholarly or popular idiom), men may well understand and apprehend.

As men communicate this good news, this message of Christ, "the **sense** and **sound** of our word must be fundamentally positive," says Barth. This is the fourth consequence of our discovery of the humanity of God. The positive character of our words, the construction of our theological posture, involves God's grace and man's gratitude, dialogue and encounter. But this positive approach does not cloud the depravity of man's nature, and must never again lead us to dwell upon man's goodness. "Man is **not** good," says Barth, and when God looks upon man, He utters in "inexorable sharpness" the "No" to man's disobedience. All theology must put this **No** at the beginning of its enterprise.

However, encourages Barth, this "No" has been taken by Jesus Christ, has been claimed, and therefore, has removed man from under its sanction. "What takes place in God's humanity," Barth explains, "is, since it includes that 'No' in itself, the **affirmation** of man (p. 60)." This, then, is to be the character of our speaking of and addressing man -- at the same time a rebel, hypocrite, a sluggard and a creature whom God "loved, loves, and will love." In Jesus Christ, God has substituted Himself for man. "And with this explanation," says Barth, "the statement that the human spirit is naturally Christian may also be valid as an obstinately joyful proclamation."

And for those who fear that such an understanding of God's humanity harbors a universalism -- all men in all times will finally be saved by God's grace -- Barth does not say "No," but offers a quick three-part response. First, we should not panic at such a notion, whatever its "possible sense or non-sense." Second, we must discover "whether the concept could not perhaps have a good meaning," in view of such passages as Colossians 1:9, which speaks of God through Christ reconciling "all things to himself." Third, "we have no theological right to set any sort of limits to the living-kindness of God which has appeared in Jesus Christ." The joy of God's love is the joy of its unfathomable depth and breadth, its inexhaustibility and its eternal endurance.

The fifth consequence of the knowledge of God's humanity is the acknowledgement of **Christendom,** the **Church.** The existence of the Church -- "of this particular people" -- is demonstrative of the humanity of God. We delight in it, we rejoice in it, wer participate in its life. And though we readily acknowledge that **"events** precede **institution,"** we must neither neglect nor renunciate our "solidarity with the Church." To criticize the Church is allowable only from within the realization that there is no salvation outside the Church. "The Church," contends Barth, "is the particular people, the congregation...the company, which through a bit of knowledge of the gracious God manifest in Jesus Christ is constituted, appointed, and called as His witness in the world (p. 63)." And though this bit of news is paltry, admits Barth, it is unconquerable because it has been established by the Holy Spirit.

Jesus Christ is what he is for God and for man, on earth and in history, as "Lord of this community, as King of this people, as Head of this body and all of its members." There can be no private Christianity, for God has revealed himself to men in Christ as a member of community. God's humanity is expressed in community through the individual, first in Jesus Christ and then in His followers. And for this reason, theology can only be done within the context of community, and never in ivory towers, or private lighthouses.

We believe the Church as the place where the crown of humanity, namely, man's fellow-humanity, may become visible in Christocentric brotherhood. Moreover, we believe it as the place where God's glory wills to dwell upon earth, that is, where humanity -- the humanity of God -- wills to assume tangible form in time and here upon earth. Here we recognize the humanity of God (p. 65).

BIBLIOGRAPHICAL NOTES

Karl Barth (1886-1968)

Biographical Sources

There are two short but most enlightening autobiographical pieces by Barth, the first consists of recorded and edited discussions John D. Godsey had with Barth in 1963, entitled, KARL BARTH'S TABLE TALKS, published by John Knox Press. The other piece is a more formal statement by Barth, entitled, HOW I CHANGED MY MIND, introduced with an epilogue by John D. Godsey (Richmond, Va.: John Knox Press, 1966). Among the several biographical studies of Barth, which range from pious rhetoric to excellent analysis, two fine works are a selection of essays by those who knew him well edited by James F. Andrews, entitled, KARL BARTH (Herder, 1969), including a comprehensive bibliography, and Thomas H. L. Parker's KARL BARTH (Grand Rapids, Mich.: Eerdmans, 1970). For the student in need of a brief but informative essay on Barth's life and thought, an excellent one by Daniel Jenkins appears under the title, "Karl Barth," in D. G. Peerman and Martin E. Marty's A HANDBOOK OF CHRISTIAN THEOLOGIANS (Cleveland: World Publ. Co., 1965).

Primary Sources

Karl Barth is generally recognized as the most important Protestant theologian of this century, and his commentary on the BOOK OF ROMANS, first appearing in 1918 in Switzerland followed by a second edition, corrected, enlarged, and revised in 1921 and four other editions by 1933, served not only to launch his career and catapult him into international prominence, but the book itself shook the Protestant world which was still enamored with 19th century theological liberalism. The English edition was translated by Edwin C. Hoskyns from the sixth German edition, THE EPISTLE TO THE ROMANS (N.Y.: Oxford University Press, 1968). The content of his commentary is that the Pauline problems in the first century, e.g., what is the relationship between the Bible and culture, between theology and religious experience, are the same kind of problems the modern Church and preacher face. Few commentaries, an exception being Luther's commentary on ROMANS, have had the influence this study has had upon Western Christianity. To read Barth's commentary on Romans is to read him at his best.

Barth's bibliography alone would fill an entire book, but for our purposes, there are a few indispensable worlds which must not go unmentioned. In 1930, the University of Glasgow awarded Barth the honorary degree of Doctor of Divinity in appreciaiton of his book entitled in translation from the German, ANSELM: FAITH IN SEARCH OF UNDERSTANDING (trans. by Ian W. Robertson, N.Y.: World Publ., 1962). Barth here scrutinizes Anselm's proofs for the existence of God, placing Anselm in his own 11th century context. Barth admits that his own theological method follows the same kind of approach as used by St. Anselm. Robert McAfee Brown has said that any student desiring to grasp Barth's theological method must understand this most "crucial work."

Not only was Barth a celebrated dogmatist, he also wrote a classic historical study of 18th and 19th century theological development entitled, DIE PROTESTANTISHE THEOLOGIE IM 19. JAHRHUNDER, Zurick, 1952 (eleven chapters being translated by Brian Cozens as PROTESTANT THOUGHT: FROM ROUSSEAU TO RITSCHEL, London, Simon and Schuster, 1969). Paul Tillich called this "my favorite among Barth's books..." Harry P. Van Dusen called it "an indispensable introduction to the most powerful and influential theological mind of this century." Of course, Barth's largest conribution to dogmatic theology in its most comprehensive form is to be found in his multi-volumed CHURCH DOGMATICS, Vols. I-IV (ed. and trans. by G. T. Thomson, G. W. Bromiley, T. F. Torrance, **et. al.**, T. and T. Clarke, Edinburgh, 1939-1960).

For the student and non-theologian, there are two single volume-editions which may prove most helpful. First is Karl Barth's DOGMATIK IM GRUNDRISS, Munchen, 1947 (trans. by G. T. Thomson, entitled, DOGMATICS IN OUTLINE, N.Y.: Harper and Row, 1959), being an excellent summary and introduction to the central themes of his system. The other study is CHURCH DOGMATICS: A SELECTION, selected and with an Introduction by Helmut Gollwitzer (trans. and edited by G. W. Bromiley, N.Y.: Harper Torchbook, 1962), which is a fine selection from Barth's CHURCH DOGMATICS gathered under such rubrics as "Revelation," "Jesus Christ," "Nothingness," and "Man and Woman." For the beginner, either or both books will prove most valuable.

Two other short works by Barth are important to mention here. Barth has written a commentary on the Apostles' Creed according to Calvin's catechism for the layman, entitled, THE FAITH OF THE CHURCH (edited by Jean-Louis Leuba, trans. by Gabriel Vahanian, N.Y.: Meridian books, 1958). Another little treasure is Karl Barth's EVANGELICAL THEOLOGY: AN INTRODUCTION (trans. by Grover Foley, Garden City, N.Y.: Doubleday Anchor, 1964), described in the words of Joseph Sittler, as "...pungent and potent essence of the man as he condenses for the common reader his understanding of what Christian theology is."

Secondary Sources

There are numerous scholarly studies of Barth's thought and to just list them would be of little profit here and would consume many pages. From a critical conservative standpoint, no better evaluation of Barth's theology exists than that of the highly respected, conservative Reformed theologian of Westminster Theological Seminary, Cornelius Van Til, entitled, THE NEW MODERNISM: AN APPRAISAL OF THE THEOLOGY OF BARTH AND BRUNNER (London: James Clarke, 1946).

From a liberal Catholic viewpoint, Hans Kung has offered a fine estimation of Barth, entitled, in translation, JUSTIFICATION: THE DOCTRINE OF KARL BARTH AND A CATHOLIC REFLECTION, with a letter by Karl Barth (trans. from the German by Thomas Collins, E. E. Tolk, and David Granskon, N.Y.: Nelson, 1964). For the beginner, a fine introduction to Barth's thought is by Herbert Hartwell, THE THEOLOGY OF KARL BARTH: AN INTRODUCTION (London: Duckworth, 1964). Two of the most scholarly treatments are: Gerrit Cornelis Berkouwer, THE TRIUMPH OF GRACE IN THE THEOLOGY OF KARL BARTH (trans. from the Dutch by Harry R. Boer, Grand Rapids, Mich.: Wm. B. Eerdmans Publ., 1956), and Hans Urs Von Balthasar, KARL BARTH: DAR STELLUNG UN DEUTUNG SEINER THEOLOGIE (trans. by John Drury as THE THEOLOGY OF KARL BARTH, N.Y.: Holt, Rinehart, Winston, 1971).

In addition to these book-length studies, there are countless essays on Barth, two of particular help to students and the common reader can be found in Hugh Ross MacKintosh's TYPES OF MODERN THEOLOGY: SCHLEIERMACHER TO BARTH (N.Y.: Charles Scribners'

Sons, 1937), Chapter VIII, "The Theology of the Word of God: Karl Barth," and in John B. Cobb, Jr.'s, LIVING OPTIONS IN PROTESTANT THEOLOGY: A SURVEY OF METHODS (Philadelphia: Westminster, 1962), Part II, "Theological Positivism," Chapter 7, "Karl Barth."

CHAPTER SEVEN

"The Spiritual Community"

"Because Christian community is founded solely on
Jesus Christ, it is spiritual and not a psychic reality.
In this it differs absolutely from all other communities."

--Dietrich Bonhoeffer (1906-1945)

Introduction

Dietrich Bonhoeffer, at the age of 39, was executed by the Nazis
in 1945 because of his outspoken involvement in the underground
"Confessing Church" in Germany. During his short life, Bonhoeffer
reached out and touched the lives of many young Germans, clergy
and laity alike. In a series of books, viz., THE COST OF DISCIPLESHIP,
ETHICS, and LIFE TOGETHER, he constructed a challenge to life
based on the high cost of following Jesus to which many chose to
respond. In LIFE TOGETHER, written just before his martyrdom,
Bonhoeffer drew up a practical guide, in devotional form, by which
the followers of Christ could live in spiritual community -- life
together in Christ. This little devotional guide is recognized as one
of the outstanding Protestant efforts at setting up a rule for community.
Its power is in its simplicity, in its piety, in its practical address to
the daily life in the spiritual community. It has rightfully become
in modern times a Christian guide for life together.*

§ § §

LIFE TOGETHER was written on the eve of World War II. During
the war, Bonhoeffer was martyred by the Nazis. Bonhoeffer's love
of the church, what he preferred to call the "spiritual community,"

---

*Unless otherwise noted, all quotations are from Bonhoeffer's LIFE
TOGETHER (1965).

led him to speak out against the growing evil he sensed among the German military leadership. Those ministers who joined Bonhoeffer in the "Confessing Church" movement got their inspiration from this little practical devotional on the Christian life expressed in community. Bonhoeffer envisioned a spiritual community wherein theological education for the ministry would occur within a communal life which took seriously Christ's call to personal discipleship. In a later work, Bonhoeffer explored in considerable detail the implications of Christ's demanding discipleship entitled, THE COST OF DISCIPLESHIP. John D. Godsey, the senior theological commentator on Bonhoeffer, has characterized LIFE TOGETHER as "simply written, powerfully convincing and unusually quotable...It is an attempt to give practical guidance to those who want to take their lives as Christians seriously."

Bonhoeffer divides life together into five distinct but related experiences. First, man is in and of community, and the Christian challenge is to spiritualize community through the discovery of Christ's meaning for man. Secondly, the life of true community is called "the day with others," which includes the demands of living not for oneself nor by oneself, but in spending the day with others -- in prayer, in meal, in work, in play. But also, in order that man might grow into spiritual wholeness, he must have time and opportunity to spend "the day alone" -- the third experience of life together. A fourth experience is a call to "ministry," a call to serve others in need, not as you personally would have others be, but minister to others as they really are in the knowledge and spirit of Christ who accepts, forgives, and loves the weak and wicked. Lastly and consummately by means of "confession," men move into true "communion," the final expression of the spiritual community. Let us examine more closely the emergence of this confessing communion from within the life together.

For too long, Christians have taken for granted the privilege of gathering undisturbed for worship and fellowship. Writing on the eve of the Nazi holocaust, Bonhoeffer warns the Christian community of the impending destruction of such privileges, and calls the Church to take stock of its blessings, to cherish them, and make them vital to its life together. No community of believers should rely on such legal rights as free assembly, for "it is by the grace of God," not of men as we too frequently suppose, "that a congregation is permitted to gather visibly in this world to share God's Word and sacrament (p. 8)."*

The people of God have never for any long period of time been able to dwell together without external attacks, or internal disruptions. And, the only power and force which can ever be relied upon to keep the community of believers together, even in their separation, is Jesus Christ himself. For by remembering Him, even those in scattered and distant lands can know and feel the spiritual life together. "This is the heavenly fellowship," says Bonhoeffer, "shared by the exile on the day of his Lord's resurrection." This sharing of the Christian community's unity by means of the Word and Sacrament is a constant source of strength to those exiled in distant places. But, for those who daily enjoy the physical presence of their brothers and sisters, "it is easily forgotten that the fellowship...is a gift of grace, a gift of the Kingdom of God..."

This gift of grace, this enduring fellowship of the physical presence of the Christian community, may at any moment be taken away, for "the measure with which God bestows the gift of visible community is varied." We must delight in our community, in the bodily presence of fellow believers. Yearning for this physical presence is no call for shame, rather a call for rejoicing. Bonhoeffer's treatise rises to eloquence in extolling the joys of fellowship, as we notice here:

> Man was created a body, the Son of God appeared on earth in the body, he was raised in the body, in the sacrament the believer receives the Lord Christ in the Body, and the resurrection of the dead will bring about the perfected fellowship of God's spiritual-physical creatures. The believer therefore lauds the Creator, the Redeemer, God, Father, Son and Holy Spirit, for the bodily presence of a brother (p. 9).

And throughout the Church, there is growing realization that this bodily presence of other fellow believers, being a grace, is to be sought after and is being sought after in ever increasing degrees of earnestness. Though it may be wrenched from us at any moment, at least for now, we must grasp it and live in its powers and might. To live together as Christians is to share all of life together, and, observed Bonhoeffer, "Communal life is again being recognized by Christians today as the grace that it is, as the extraordinary, the 'roses and lilies' of the Christian life."

When characterizing this community of life together as Christian, it must never be forgotten that such a community can come into being and continue to exist only as its life is centered in and through Jesus Christ. "Whether it be a brief, single encounter or the daily fellowship of years, Christian community is only this," i.e., life together in Jesus Christ. Furthermore, "we belong to one another," explains Bonhoeffer, "only through and in Jesus Christ." This awareness of Christ's centrality to the experience of life together in community has three interrelated meanings. First, it means that "a Christian needs others because of Jesus Christ." The Christian, because of his knowledge of God's grace offered through Jesus, no longer seeks himself, his own interest, or salvation. His life, as his death, is at the disposition of God in Christ; he lives wholly "by the truth of God's Word in Jesus Christ," and not by his own thoughts and deeds. But since God "has put this Word into the mouth of men in order that it may be communicated to other men," all men, including and especially Christians, need other Christians who speak God's Word to them. "The goal of all Christian community," is this, says Bonhoeffer, that "they meet one another as bringers of the message of salvation (p. 12)." This meeting is a gift of God's grace, and the community of Christians which springs forth does so because of this eternal message of the "justification of man through grace alone..."

A second meaning of the awareness that Christian community is possible only through and in Jesus Christ is that "a Christian comes to others only through Jesus Christ." This is so because of the depravity and discord of and between men devoid of God's grace made known through Jesus Christ. "Without Christ," explains Bonhoeffer, "there is discord between God and man and between man and man (p. 12)." Without the mediatorial role of Jesus, man would not know God as personal and neither would he know man as brother. Christ has made peace with God and offered salvation to men. Without Christ, in whom the Christian gives his will up for that of God's, men cannot know each other as brother because of man's personal ego -- that blocking force which serves to separate men in community. But in Christ we become one with God and one with man. Therefore, through God's love spread abroad in the hearts of men by Christ, community is possible.

And thirdly, community exists through and in Jesus Christ because only "in Jesus Christ have we been chosen from eternity, accepted in time, and united for eternity." Because of this Divine grace God is not where men are not, where He is man is by virtue of the Incarnation, on the Cross, and in the Resurrection. But since we have been chosen by Him from the beginning and for eternity, we are so **together!** Salvation, then, is not singular but plural, not individual but social, not separate but collective. And this being chosen by God through Jesus Christ revealed to us as our Brother has constituted "the beginning of our instruction in divine love (p. 13)." Saint John has said in the Golden Scripture Text, "God so loved the world that He gave His only begotten Son..." Since we are recipients of that Divine Love, we are obliged to share it with others.

This sense of the brotherhood of all mankind comes only through the sharing of God's love offered through Jesus, for, says Bonhoeffer, "One is a brother to another only through Jesus Christ." The brotherhood of man does not derive from what men are in themselves. "What determines our brotherhood," explains Bonhoeffer, "is what that man is by reason of Christ (p. 14)." Only when men come to know of Christ is community possible, for without knowledge of Christ, men do not know of their brotherhood with other men nor of their saved state in God's grace. Only Christ can show man who he is and what he can become. Bonhoeffer cautions against the dangers awaiting those seeking community who desire something more than life together in Christ. For those "looking for some extraordinary social experience (are) bringing muddled and impure desires into Christian brotherhood," and must be inevitably disappointed.

There are two characteristics of Christian brotherhood which must appear at the outset if community is to be realized. **"First, that Christian brotherhood is not an ideal but a divine reality. Second, that Christian brotherhood is a spiritual and not a psychic reality** (p. 15)." Bonhoeffer is not optimistic about the capacity of man to actualize the communal life together by means of a "wish dream." The spiritual community which comes through life in Jesus Christ is not derived from man, but from God. And when dreamers foist their visions upon the community of Christ, these visions become a serious hindrance to the spiritual community. To know the love of God revealed in Christ is to understand that God's grace "does not abandon us to those rapturous experiences and lofty moods that come over us like a dream (p. 15)." If man is destined to live under his own dreams, he is doomed to perpetual disillusionment.

The Christian community is derived from God, and thus, men are responsible for responding to the Divine love from whence has come the presencing of God among men in Jesus. If the community looks to another source for its life together other than in God, the community is confronted with the depravity of man apart from grace, the egoism of man apart from divine love. "The man who fashions a visionary ideal of community," explains Bonhoeffer, "demands that it be realized by God, by others, and by himself." The danger lurking amidst the dreams and visions of men in search of community devoid of an awareness of God's grace revealed in Jesus is that once men attempt to implement the human dream and fail, they become accusers, they lay blame for failure upon their brethren, upon God, and upon themselves. But where men fail, God in Christ can redeem, where men fall short of their petty dreams, God can rise up, and when men turn and accuse themselves and their fellows, God offers salvation and forgiveness. "When the morning mists of dreams vanish," says Bonhoeffer, "then dawns the bright day of Christian fellowship (p. 17)." Men cannot lay personal claim to the spiritual community in any possessive sense, for the community's life together is not dependent upon men's efforts and dreams, work and visions, but solely upon Christ. Men must pray, sing, and labor, but God gives life to the spiritual community.

Not only is Christian brotherhood a divine reality and not an ideal, but it is also a spiritual reality rather than a psychic reality. This is so because the community is founded upon Jesus Christ, and not upon thoughts and ideas derived from the human psyche, or human spirit. Bonhoeffer spends much time in contrasting the spiritual community and the human community -- spiritual reality versus human reality. Whereas "the basis of all spiritual reality is the clear, manifest Word of God in Jesus Christ, the basis of all human reality is the dark turbid urges and desires of the human mind (p. 19)." To forget this qualitative difference between the human and the spiritual is to invite disillusionment and despair upon any attempt at community. **Truth** is to the spiritual community what **desire** is to the human community. The "light of Christ" is the essence of the spiritual community whereas the "darkness of evil men" is the essence of the human community. The fellowship of those "who are called by Christ" occurs in the community of the Spirit, but the fellowship of those who are devout souls called into community by desire is in the human community. In the former is order and brotherly service **(agape)**, but in the latter only "disordered desire for pleasure (eros)."

A community based on human love is destined to demise, because "human love has little regard for truth," human love is petty and self serving, resulting in jealousy and spite. Men cannot count on community surviving on a love derived from man. The spiritual community lives on love centered in and derived from Jesus Christ -- a pure, spiritual love from whence all strength in community must come. This Divine Love is untainted by human depravity, and to live in this love is to share with others the joy of spiritual community based upon Christ's love in and for us, not upon man's love in and for himself.

This love of God does not originate in my brother or my enemy, but in God Himself. Furthermore, this love stands between me and my brothers and enemies holding us together through the grace offered in Christ. I do not confront and love my brother and enemy directly, but rather through the mediation of Jesus Christ. "This means," explains Bonhoeffer, "that I must release the other person from every attempt of mine to regulate, coerce, and dominate him with my love... Because Christ has long since acted decisively for my brother...I must leave him his freedom to be Christ's...(23)."

This is the test of spiritual love -- everything it does and says must commend Christ. Human love is controlled and guided by dark **desires** of depraved and lost men; spiritual love thrives in the light of Christ ordered in the service of brotherhood and **truth**. The challenge to the Christian life together is this, "the ability to distinguish between a human ideal and God's reality, between spiritual and human community." The experience of Christian brotherhood is a gift of God's grace, and it is not promised to all. And though the joy of such experience is great and is to be sought after, nevertheless, we must never forget that "it is not the experience of Christian brotherhood, but solid and certain faith in brotherhood that holds us together...We are bound together by faith, not by experience...For Jesus Christ alone is our unity...Through him alone we do have access to one another, joy in one another, and fellowship with one another."

The practical life together in the spiritual community is a life spent immersed in the daily affairs of one's brothers and sisters. "The day with others," as Bonhoeffer called it, is a day filled with work and play, prayer and song. "Communal life under the Word," says Bonhoeffer, "begins with common worship at the beginning of the day (p. 28)." If we as a "family community" are to grow in our knowledge of Christ's presence among us, it must be done together -- in praise and thanks, in the reading of Scripture, in prayer. Whenever the community gathers for collective devotion, there should be included "the word of Scripture, the hymns of the Church, and the prayer of the fellowship."

Bonhoeffer insists that the reading of the Psalter is a vital expression of spiritual health. From the earliest of time, the Church has valued the Psalter, using it as a means of collective prayers. Today, we understand it to be the praying of Christ Himself through the mouth of His Church. "The Psalter is the vicarious prayer of Christ for his Church," says Bonhoeffer, and by using it, the Church learns to pray "on the basis of Christ's prayer (p. 32)." We learn three things about prayer specifically from the Psalter -- first, we learn that prayer means "praying according to the Word of God, on the basis of promises;" second, "we learn from the prayer of the psalms what we should pray;" and third, "the psalms teach us to pray as a fellowship -- (we) learn to pray the prayer of the Body of Christ."

Besides the Psalter, the family community must give attendance to the reading of the Holy Scriptures. "As a whole," counsels Bonhoeffer, "The Scriptures are God's revealing Word. Only in the infiniteness of its inner relationships...will the full witness to Jesus Christ the Lord be perceived (p. 36)." Through the reading of Scripture, we are transported from present profane time and are "set down in the midst of the holy history of God on earth." It is there that God dealt with men of old and there He will deal with us -- we share our needs and confess our sins, we learn of His judgment and of His eternal grace. In Scripture, the mystery of Jesus is made known to the faithful -- to the unbeliever a tragic story but to the believer a divine truth. And in the reading of Holy Scripture, says Bonhoeffer, "we learn to know our own history."

Following the prayers of the psalter and the reading of Holy Scripture, the family community should sing together -- "this being the voice of the Church, praising, thanking, and praying." Though the Word communicated in the hymn is the focus of our attention, for the music is "completely the servant of the Word," nevertheless, the joy of life together in Christ cannot be adequately spoken; it must be sung. This unison singing is not so much a musical as a spiritual matter. The individual voice is not important, for the hymn is not that of an individual, but that of the whole Church. "It is the voice of the Church that is heard in singing together...it is the Church that is singing, and you, as a member of the Church, may share in its song (p. 45)."

Common prayer is an indispensable experience in the life together. In addition to reading the prayers of the Psalter, we must also say our own prayers. "We are to pray to God as a fellowship, and this prayer must really be our word, our prayer for this day, for our work, for our fellowship, for the particular needs and sins that oppress us in common, for the persons who are committed to our care (p. 45)." Common prayer is the expression of faith in God, its love of Christ, and its dedication to the Church. This praying together establishes and witnesses to the faith of the spiritual community in God, the Source of its strength, the Securer of its life. This prayer must be a free flowing expression of love and obedience -- not forced due to ritual, but dynamic because of faith. Ceremony and ritual become customary ways whereby the Church expresses its faith; the community becomes habituated to prayer and singing -- a sacred habit! Man is an animal of habit, and no greater habit for Christ's sake exists than common prayer.

The day with others not only must include common worship, it must also involve "the fellowship of the table." After feeding on the Bread of Life in worship together, the family community comes together to feast upon God's earthly bread. "Ever since Jesus Christ sat at table with his disciples," says Bonhoeffer, "the table fellowship of his community has been blessed with his presence (p. 49)." There are three distinct kinds of table fellowship which Jesus keeps with the community: the daily fellowship at table, the table fellowship of the Lord's Supper, and the final table fellowship in the Kingdom of God. In daily fellowship, I come to know my unity with my brethren for the bread that we share is not my own but ours. In the Lord's Supper, I come again to the knowledge of God's love for me and us revealed in the life of Christ now expressed through community. The hope of today will be realized in the great coming of Christ to claim his own, wherein all will partake of the Bread of Life.

The day with others is spent not only in worship, but also and mostly in labor. Though the first moments of every day are spent in common worship, the large part of every day is spent apart from the communal fellowship in day labor. Worship and work are two distinct activities of the members of community, and only after each activity is respected for itself alone will it become clear that they are "inseparably together." As the Christian plunges himself into the world of things, he necessarily steps out of the world of brotherly encounter, but beyond the thing itself is God who blesses all things in their order. As men immerse themselves in work, leaving their egos behind with all their fleshly desires, they can come into contact with the "Thou" beyond the "It." By so doing, work becomes "a means of liberation" from oneself. And when this breakthrough occurs, from the It to the Thou, work and prayer are united. The Christian does not cease from prayer in work, nor from working in prayer. By such an insight, "the whole day acquires an order and a discipline."

"A day at a time is long enough to sustain one's faith," says Bonhoeffer, and both the noontime meal and evening gathering are opportunities for rest and fellowship. The Christian does not take for granted the profits of his labors, rather he rejoices in and praises God for His grace. At the close of day, we thank God for His blessings, and pray God's blessings upon the safety of all Christendom, upon all men, and upon our spiritual community. The petition for forgiveness of sins rightly comes at the end of the day -- realizing our weaknesses and wickednesses yet rejoicing in God's loving kindness and the joy found in the forgiveness offered through Christ Jesus. And though we are to sleep and rest for the coming of tomorrow's labor, we "pray that when our eyes are closed in sleep, God may nevertheless keep our hearts awake (p. 56)." And when the dawn comes, each member of the spiritual community rises to begin life anew -- in prayer, Scripture, and song.

Life together also involves for the individual an opportunity to spend "the day alone." Let not he who thinks that true community means simply unending companionship seek it out in order to escape his own loneliness. He who is afraid of his own loneliness will not fare well in true community. A community devoid of times for solitude for its members is not a truly spiritual community -- "The Christian community is not a spiritual sanatorium," counsels Bonhoeffer, "the person who comes into a fellowship because he is running away from himself is misusing it for the sake of diversion." Those who are seeking a cure from the fear of their own solitude are not ready for community -- "resignation and spiritual death are the result of such attempts to find a cure."

"**Let him who cannot be alone beware of community.**" Only harm can come from one who cannot abide his aloneness, for in one's solitude, you stand before God. If I cannot stand before God in my solitude, I cannot endure the company of His faithful. In my aloneness, I must stand before God, I must hear and answer His call, I must struggle and pray, and in my aloneness before God, I must die and give an accounting. To try to escape from myself is foolishness, for neither can God be hidden from. "If you refuse to be alone," warns Bonhoeffer, "you are rejecting Christ's call to you, and you can have no part in the community of those who are called (p. 58)." The spiritual community must beware -- Let him who cannot be alone beware of community.

But, the reverse is equally true. "**Let him who is not in community beware of being alone.**" The Christian has been called into community. Man is not saved by and unto himself, he is called from out of human community into spiritual community. Christ's Body is the Church Catholic and Apostolic. "If you scorn the fellowship of the brethren, you reject the call of Jesus Christ," says Bonhoeffer, "and thus your solitude can only be hurtful to you." The spiritual community is the arena for the joyful proclamation of God's grace to man. The Church is the voice of God in its singing, praying, and testifying. And he who would know the true meaning of solitude must know the meaning of spiritual community, and he who would know true community must come to know true solitude. "Both begin at the same time," says Bonhoeffer, "namely, with the call of Jesus Christ."

The balance to "the day with others" is "the day alone." Accompanying the joyous day of Christian family fellowship is "the lonely day of the individual." Each must have the other to be whole and complete. Solitude and silence have meaning in the context of community and fellowship. "The mark of solitude is silence," says Bonhoeffer, "as speech is the mark of community (and their interdependence is seen when we realize that) right speech comes out of silence, and right silence comes out of speech."

This silence within which and out of which true community dwells and speaks is not some vague "ceremonial gesture" or "mystical desire to get beyond the Word." Such a notion is wrong-headed, and militates against the spirit of community. "Silence," says Bonhoeffer, "is the simple stillness of the individual under the Word of God (p. 29)." That silence which is for the strengthening and building up of community is the silence which arises out of an encounter with God's Word -- men are speechless before it! At the day's beginning, we are silent for the hearing of God's Word first, as we are silent at the day's ending in order that we might hear God's Word last. Such silence is derived from a "spiritual stillness" which must characterize man's posture towards God's Word.

There are three purposes for which the Christian must seek a time to spend the day alone: Scripture meditation, prayer, and intercession. Scripture meditation is not a time for experimentation, nor a time to seek out the dark recesses of our feeble minds, as if such an activity merited the effort. What is there to man worthy of such exploration except God's grace which is given through Christ? "The time of meditation does not let us down into the void and abyss of loneliness; it lets us be alone with the Lord." And by pondering in solitude the day's message, we encounter God afresh in the moment alone. And from such an encounter, we rise to face the day.

The meditation upon Scripture naturally leads to prayer, guided by and based upon the Word. "According to a word of Scripture," says Bonhoeffer, "we pray for the clarification of our day, for preservation from sin, for growth in sanctification, for faithfulness and strength in our work (p. 64)." And thirdly, a Christian's solitude is for the intercessary prayers, the naming of dear ones, of those so close to one's heart, so near the life of community. The naming of names is itself a means of grace -- to call out the name of one for whom we wish God's favor, attention, and blessing. "A Christian fellowship," explains Bonhoeffer, "lives and exists by the intercession of its members for one another, or it collapses." The strength of community is measured in terms of each member's concern for others, those departed, sick, or grieved in body, mind, and spirit. To call another's name in prayer is to evoke God's blessing on both.

Within every social grouping of people, no less the spiritual community, there eventually arises the question of leadership. And so that the spiritual community might avoid the perennial pitfalls of human communities living under the weight of this oligarchic imperative, Bonhoeffer directs the community to a variety of ministries which should stifle the will to power and create an atmosphere of communal ministry.

One form of vital ministry to the community Bonhoeffer calls, "the ministry of holding one's tongue." Evil thoughts inevitably come to weak and sinful men, even to the most spiritually travelled among us, but such thoughts are usually most effectively dealt with by not giving wind to them, i.e., not saying them aloud. "Thus it might be a decisive rule of every Christian fellowship," suggests Bonhoeffer, "that each individual is prohibited from saying much that occurs to him (p. 70)." Such a rule would encourage men to suspend judgment against a brother, to be less critical, less scrutinizing. After all, no man stands justified except and solely by God's grace in Jesus Christ. Who am I that I should condemn or judge, being condemned and judged myself already apart from Christ's love.

Another form of ministry is the ministry of meakness. "Only he who lives by the forgiveness of his sin in Jesus Christ," says Bonhoeffer, "will rightly think little of himself. He will know that his own wisdom reached the end of its tether when Jesus forgave (p. 73)." Only after I come to know of my salvation solely in and through Divine grace will I be willing to accept even unfair insults and injuries. Without the ministry of meekness, a community is doomed to an egotist's death of self-pride.

A third ministry is that of listening. This is the first responsibility one has towards others in community, viz., to listen. "Just as love of God begins with listening to his Word," says Bonhoeffer, "so the beginning of love for the Brethren is learning to listen to them." Pastoral care is to listening what the Word is to preaching -- "We should listen with the ears of God that we may speak the Word of God." The ministry of helpfulness -- "We must be ready to allow ourselves to be interrupted by God" -- is followed by the ministry of bearing. Bearing means forebearing and sustaining, and a Christian can bear with another because Christ has borne the burdens of us all. The mercy of the Christian community is namely this, though the Christian must bear another's burden, he does not need to judge. Christ has freed us all from both judging and being judged.

"What a difficult thing it often is," confesses Bonhoeffer, "to utter the name of Jesus Christ in the presence even of a brother." And so, the need for the ministry of proclaiming, not by clergy alone, but by all believers. The gift of proclamation comes with the realiza-tion that we are all sinners, and in spite of our human dignity, we are all lonely and lost and in need of help. And only after all of these ministries are employed -- of hearing, helping, bearing, and proclaim-ing, can we hope to find the ministry of genuine spiritual authority. Such authority can exist only in an atmosphere of deep reverence for the centrality of Christ in community, for such authority knows that it is bound by the words of Jesus, "One is your Master, even Christ, and all ye are brethren (Matt.23: 8)."

Bonhoeffer concludes his study of the life together by considering the nature and place of confession and communion in the life of the spiritual community. For though the Christian may engage in corporate worship, common prayer, and all facets of communal fellowship, "the final break-through to fellowship does not occur, because, though they have fellowship with one another as believers and as devout people, they do not have fellowship as the undevout, as sinners (p. 86)." True fellowship comes when we move beyond a shallow piety of self-righteousness to a deep sense of our sinful nature yet saved condition in Christ. "The misery of the sinner and the mercy of God -- this was the truth of the Gospel in Jesus Christ." Through the power of the Incarnation, Christ presents himself in community by means of the individual. And thus, says Bonhoeffer, in a true sense, "when I go to my brother to confess, I am going to God."

Confession implies certain breakthroughs, for the individual and for community. First, confession results in the breakthrough to community, for whereas sin demands to have man by himself alone, community brings the individual into itself by means of confession. "In confession," Bonhoeffer explains, "the light of the Gospel breaks into the darkness and seclusion of the heart (and) since the confession of sin is made in the presence of a Christian brother, the last stronghold of self-justification is abandoned." In addition to the breakthrough to community, in confession there is also a breakthrough to the Cross. "The root of all sin is pride," says Bonhoeffer. But by confessing our sins, we strip away pride, face the scandal of the Cross, and accept its burden as our own. And by so doing, our old man of sin dies, and we are enabled to "share in the resurrection of Christ and eternal life (p. 90)."

Another breakthrough made possible by confession is to New Life. We break with sin in confession, and where this break is, there is conversion. Old things pass away, our New Life in the Spirit begins -- "Confession is discipleship." "What happened to us in baptism," explains Bonhoeffer, "is bestowed upon us anew in confession." And thus, the final breakthrough is to certainty -- "A man who confesses his sins in the presence of a brother knows that he is no longer alone with himself; he experiences the presence of God in the reality of the other person (p. 91)." This certainly is God's gift of abiding grace to the spiritual community. This certainty is witnessed to in the ultimate expression of life together, viz., in Holy Communion. The day of the Lord's Supper is a day of joyful fellowship -- Christ is come!

The fellowship of the Lord's Supper is the superlative fulfillment of Christian fellowship. As the members of the congregation are united in body and blood at the table of the Lord so will they be together in eternity. Here the community has reached its goal. Here joy in Christ and his community is complete. The life of Christians together under the Word has reached its perfection in the sacrament (p. 96).

BIBLIOGRAPHICAL NOTE

Dietrich Bonhoeffer (1906-1945)

Biographical Sources

There are several really fine biographies of Bonhoeffer, ranging from the light but informative to the indepth study of the personality and times of Bonhoeffer. The most valuable autobiographical materials on Bonhoeffer have appeared as collections of his personal letters, many from prison. Two excellent collections are, LETTERS AND PAPERS FROM PRISON (edited by Eberhard Bethge, trans. by Reginald H. Fuller, N.Y.: Macmillan, 1962), a small but challenging collection of Bonhoeffer's thought during his prison stay awaiting execution on the Nazi gallows, and TRUE PATRIOTISM: LETTERS, LECTURES, AND NOTES (1939-1945), (edited with introduction by Edwin H. Robertson, N.Y.: Harper and Row, 1973), with excellent bibliography which constitutes a substantial collection of autobiographically important documents.

Of the numerous biographies of Bonhoeffer, several merit mentioning. Sabine Leibholz-Bonhoeffer has given a comprehensive insight into the family from which Bonhoeffer came, entitled, THE BONHOEFFERS: PORTRAIT OF A FAMILY (London: Sidgwick and Jackson, 1971), while Wolf D. Zimmermann has gathered biographical statements from those who knew Bonhoeffer best as friend, minister, and colleague, entitled, I KNEW DIETRICH BONHOEFFER (London: Collins, 1966). A captivating and exhaustive inquiry into Bonhoeffer's life and martyrdom has been written by Mary Bosanquet, entitled, THE LIFE AND DEATH OF DIETRICH BONHOEFFER: MAN OF VISION, MAN OF COURAGE (trans. from German by Eric Mosbacher, editorship of Edwin Robertson, N.Y.: Harper and Row, 1970).

A somewhat more theologically oriented biography, with introduction by Robert McAfee Brown, appeared during the same year by Andre Dumas, entitled, DIETRICH BONHOEFFER, THEOLOGIAN OF REALITY (N.Y.: Macmillan, 1970), which has a good selected bibliography.

A shorter and lighter work is by Theodore A. Gill, entitled, MEMO FOR A MOVIE: A SHORT LIFE OF DIETRICH BONHOEFFER (N.Y.: Macmillan, 1971). A study of Bonhoeffer's life as a resistance leader and underground clergyman has been written by Larry L. Rasmussen, entitled, DIETRICH BONHOEFFER: REALITY AND RESISTANCE (Nashville: Abingdon Press, 1972). For the student and lay reader in search of a short but well written biography of Bonhoeffer, Dallas M. Roark has written such a book for the MAKERS OF THE MODERN THEOLOGICAL MIND series, entitled, DIETRICH BONHOEFFER (Waco, Texas: Word Books, 1972).

Primary Sources

The book which catapulted Bonhoeffer into national and international prominence as a serious theological scholar was his NACHFOLGE, Munich, 1937 (trans. by R. H. Fuller as THE COST OF DISCIPLESHIP, N.Y.: Macmillan, 1968), a book Samuel H. Miller of Harvard characterized as "a powerful attack on 'easy Christianity'..." The demands of the Christian life are made explicit in this struggle of man in the world seeking after God -- the costs are great, but the rewards of true discipleship are greater. The following year, Bonhoeffer wrote GEMEINSAMES LEBEN, Munich, 1938 (trans. by J. W. Doberstein as LIFE TOGETHER, London: SCM, 1965), which is an exploration of the meaning and possibilities of community conceived in Christian terms -- the Christing of community. Bonhoeffer's ETHIK, Munich, 1949 (trans. by N. H. Smith, N.Y.: Macmillan, 1965), is recognized as one of the most rigorously constructed and consistently systematic explications of Christian ethics in the 20th century. The root and ground of Christian ethics is in the reality of God as revealed in Jesus Christ. The Church and State are not separate, for the Christian must live this reality of Christ in all parts of his personal and social life.

In addition to the several editions of published letters, mentioned earlier, Bonhoeffer has four more little books of importance for us here: CHRIST THE CENTER (N.Y.: Harper and Row, 1966), an explication of his christology; COMMUNION OF SAINTS (N.Y.: Harper and Row, 1964), a further elaboration of his understanding of Christian's life together; CREATION AND FALL (N.Y.: Macmillan, 1964), being an inquiry into the nature of man in the world and his relationships to himself, his fellowman, and the environment; and I LOVE THIS PEOPLE (N.Y.: John Knox, 1965), an expression of Bonhoeffer's pastoral love for men most unloveable.

Secondary Sources

Without question, John D. Godsey's study of Bonhoeffer's theology is the most comprehensive study available, entitled, THE THEOLOGY OF DIETRICH BONHOEFFER (Philadelphia: Westminster Press, 1960), including an exhaustive bibliography of primary sources. A somewhat more recent study, with significant complements to Godsey's study as well as some uniquely provocative insights of its own, is that of John A. Phillips, entitled, CHRIST FOR US IN THE THEOLOGY OF DIETRICH BONHOEFFER (N.Y.: Harper and Row, 1967). Though heavily oriented towards Bonhoeffer's christology, the work can serve as a responsible overview of his whole system. Another overview of Bonhoeffer's theology as it relates to the intellectual movement of the Church during the recent past is that of the distinguished Swiss theologian-philosopher, Heinrich Ott, entitled, REALITY AND FAITH: THE THEOLOGICAL LEGACY OF DIETRICH BONHOEFFER (Philadelphia: Fortress, 1972). One last substantive treatment, especially as it explores the orthodox and innovative character of Bonhoeffer's thought is that of James W. Woelfel, entitled, Bonhoeffer's THEOLOGY: CLASSICAL AND REVOLUTIONARY (Nashville: Abingdon, 1970).

Ronald Gregor Smith has collected several essays on various aspects of Bonhoeffer's thought from such theological noteworthies as William Hamilton, Bethge, Barth, R. Prenter, H. Muller, H. Schmidt, and R. Bultmann, in a book entitled, WORLD COME OF AGE (Philadelphia: Fortress Press, 1967). Two theologians, Jurgen Moltmann and Jurgen Weissbach, have written a book on Bonhoeffer together but from two interestingly different vantage points, entitled, TWO STUDIES IN THE THEOLOGY OF BONHOEFFER (introduction and trans. by R. H. Fuller, N.Y.: Scribners', 1967). For the student interested in a quick exposure to Bonhoeffer's thought, Benjamin A. Reist has written a little study for the Promise of Theology series, entitled, THE PROMISE OF BONHOEFFER (Philadelphia: Lippencott, 1969). An even briefer but not irresponsible exposure can be gotten by reading Franklin Sherman's chapter on Bonhoeffer in D. G. Peerman and M. E. Marty (eds.), A HANDBOOK OF CHRISTIAN THEOLOGIANS (N.Y.: The World Publ., 1965).

CHAPTER EIGHT

"Faith in the Future"

"Life can progress on our planet in the future ... by
throwing down the barriers which still wall off human
activity, and by giving itself up without hesitation to
faith in the future."

--Teilhard de Chardin (1881-1955)

Introduction

No religious thinker in the 20th century has caused more discussion
and provoked more debate over the relationship between religion
and science than has the Jesuit paleontologist Pierre Teilhard de
Chardin. Once censored by the Roman Catholic Church for "dangerous"
ideas, now Teilhard is read and studied in every major center of religious thought in the Western world. Called by England's **Blackfriars,**
"the greatest synthetic thinker since St. Thomas Aquinas," Teilhard
has attempted the astounding feat of synthesizing the Christian faith
and modern science. Teilhard, author of over two dozen books and
several book editions of personal letters, will be considered in this
essay in a collection of a few short essays of his entitled, BUILDING
THE EARTH.* The challenge Teilhard chose to respond to in his career
as both priest and scientist was that of incorporating the reality of
evolution into the modern undertanding of Christ and the Church,
realizing that the theory of evolution has come to inform all of the
natural sciences. The ascent of man from out of the inorganic primordial dust of eons past was no accident, explains Teilhard. Rather,
there is purpose and direction in the universe and the evolution of
the human species with the cerebral explosion that has only recently
begun is all part of the Divine Plan -- a process of evolution that's
focused upon the Cosmic Christ. Teilhard contends that "the world

---

*Unless otherwise noted, all quotations are from Teilhard's BUILDING
THE EARTH (1969).

would not function, if there were not, somewhere outside time and space, a cosmic point of total synthesis." Teilhard understands that only through "a great hope, in common" can the earth move towards greater actualization of its potential. The challenge for modern man, if "life (is to) progress on our planet in the future..." is "without hesitation to...(establish a) faith in the future." The ultimate question of meaning is phrased by Teilhard in a typically evolutionary manner: "Is there not now underway one further metamorphosis, the ultimate one, the passage of the circles to their common Center, the realization of God at the heart of the Noosphere, the apparition of the Theosphere?"

§ § §

From a quiet aristocratic home life in central France to a challenging and exciting Jesuit novitiate on the rock-strewn Isles of Jersey, from the windswept deserts of Siberia to the electrifying ethos of Paris' Institute Catholique, Pierre Teilhard de Chardin has emerged in the last quarter of the 20th century as the single most important Christian scientist to address optimistically the coming dialogue between religion and science, Christianity and evolution. Teilhard has gone from the obscurity of a China-based paleontologist of the 1920's to one of the most highly acclaimed philosophical thinkers of the mid-20th century. During his intellectually formative years, few outside a close circle of friends knew of the genius of Teilhard's mind. Regularly and consistently refused the right to publish his philosophical and theological writings by the Church authorities in Rome who feared "heretical implications," Teilhard, though never failing in his loyalty to the Church and the Society of Jesus, was led to give his essays to a friend in Paris, Mlle. Jean Mortier. After Teilhard's death, Easter Day, 1955, Mlle. Mortier released the manuscripts for publication, and the whirlwind of excitement and enthusiasm over Teilhard's thought has subsequently been nothing less than phenomenal.

No longer feared and scrutinized as a potentially dangerous man to the orthodoxy of the Christian Church, Teilhard has gained such renown as to make him indispensable to any serious study of contemporary philosophy of man and to the dialogue between Christianity and science. Bernard Towers of England's **Blackfriars** has characterized Teilhard's thought as "the most significant achievement in synthetic thinking since that of Aquinas," Sir Julian Huxley adding that "because Teilhard's is a true vision, it not only vivifies but liberates.' The author of more than 20 books -- none of which were published until after his death -- his thought is now studied in every major intellectual center in Western civilization, as well as in Japan. Today, there are national organizations for the study of his thought in more than 25 countries with major research centers located in Paris, London, and New York City.

Within a synthetic vision of man in the world, Teilhard looked deep into the conditions of modern man and found a basis for hope in the possibility of human unity and peace. The structure of such hope is built upon a scheme that finds divine purpose in the scientifically established processes of cosmic evolution. From the primordial dust of prehistoric beginnings to the coming of modern man, Teilhard perceives a direction and purpose in the evolutionary process which has produced man who has become the mind of the earth. There is no contradiction between good science, i.e., "analysis," and Christianity, i.e., "synthesis," explains Teilhard.

Arguing from the data of paleontology while standing in the archeological digs of Eastern China, Teilhard was confident that the emergence of the human mind, of love, of community, were neither happenstance nor mathematical coincidence. Rather, this emergence of man as the topmost leaf in the tree of evolution is demonstrative of the tendency of all things to "rise and converge." From the **geosphere** (rocky earth of prelife) to the **biosphere** (greening and populating of the planet) to the **noosphere** (human consciousness as self-reflective awareness), the earth is moving toward an ultimate actualization of its potential which is now being realized through the agency of the human mind.

The final stage of evolution is the **theosphere** wherein all things come into the personal and loving care of God. Christ is the power force for this tendency toward the Divine, for by the Incarnation, God has fused His life into the life of the earth. The "christification" process is the awakening of man and matter to the reality of Christ. "All things that rise converge," says Teilhard, and the ultimate convergence is in God. "Our task," Teilhard said, "is to harness the energies of love to aid the evolutionary process and bring it to completion." "Love," says Teilhard, "is a sacred reserve of energy, and the very blood stream of spiritual evolution."

THE PHENOMENON OF MAN and THE DIVINE MILIEU are the most highly acclaimed of Telhard's works, the former a scientific, and the latter a devotional treatise on the Divine nature of cosmic evolution. Nevertheless, given their size and depth, few untrained Teilhardians can grasp the profundity of these works unaided. However, a small collection of rather brief but lucid and eloquent essays by Teilhard, entitled, BUILDING THE EARTH, constitutes the best and most jargon-free exposition of his ideas. Max Begouen's "forward" along with John Kobler's introductory essay entitled, "The Priest Who Haunts the Catholic World," are excellent introductions to Teilhard's essays in this small book.

Our concern here will be a close and careful analysis of the few short essays by Teilhard himself as we search for the nature of meaning in his thought. There is no recurrent theme so common nor topic so frequently discussed as that of the future of man. And the drive of Teilhard to demonstrate the inevitable convergence of every possible truth often led him to attempted syntheses of what on the surface appeared to be mutually alien if not outright hostile subjects.

One of the best illustrations of this point is his somewhat controversial perspective on democracy, communism, and fascism, i.e., an attempt to ferret out the deep complementary truths of what are normally considered mutually exclusive ideologies. Though his success or failure in such an endeavor is much debated, nevertheless, the attempted synthesis bespeaks his sincere belief that truth rises, and that all "that rises must converge." The "besetting temptation of our time," observes Teilhard, is a too quick willingness to adopt a defeatist attitude toward the world. It is too easy to "find an excuse for inaction," says Teilhard, "by pleading the decadence of civilization, or even the imminent end of the world (p. 49)." Man must not dwell upon his all too obvious depravity, his animality, but must press on towards the future, a future wherein man arises as he grows in love and truth.

The first and greatest challenge to modern man is that of affirming "a robust faith in the destiny of man." Without such faith, man is destined to self-pity, self flagellation and eventually self-destruction. Today, in spite of and often because of the human classes and sufferings which so readily characterize modern experience, we are seeing the emergence of "a fresh kind of life," a life centered upon and vivified by the realization that mankind "is not an accidental phenomenon" resulting from arbitrary mathematical happenstances of molecular movements. No, says Teilhard, this new life spirit which is beginning to fill the hearts of perceptive people is in recognition that "mankind represents the culmination of the whole movement of matter and life (p. 50)." Such recognition is the result of, and not in spite of, scientific discoveries about the origin of the human species. One cannot read the "chart of facts," argues Teilhard -- geologist, paleontologist, and paleo-anthropologist -- without making this great discovery.

Thanks to science, says Teilhard, the religious man, the Christian, can rejoice in the scientifically demonstrable Biblical testimony that "the work of creation is a grand design of a Personal Being," the giver of direction and purpose to evolution. Man has now come to see himself as the "finished prototype" which puts into perspective all that has gone before man and has become the foundation upon which man has evolved. And in such a perspective, man is in a position to better understand "his title to the sovereignty of the universe."

Lest one misunderstand Teilhard to be doing nothing more than contemporizing the old anthropocentrism of man as geometric center of the universe, Teilhard is quick to point out that his processual vision of man and his place in the world -- not as center but as focal point -- carries with it profound ethical and moral implications. And such a position makes our activities, and the socio-political agencies of our activities, subject to an ethic based upon cosmic evolution. The political-social changes of today speak of the crisis of progress. "We are progressing," says Teilhard, "this we can and must believe."

And yet, says he, the disorder and chaos which so often characterize the profound depths of human society today decry an absence of progress, of order and direction. "There are three major influences," Teilhard argues, "confronting each other and struggling for possession of the earth (p. 51)." They are Democracy, Communism, Fascism (all forms of authoritarian nationalism). How can anyone propose that these three world-forces are or can be positively related in the face of the global struggles that characterize their relationship?

The answer must come by way of an examination of the source of their strength. In spite of their supposed and real conflicting differences, they each in a unique and positively important way exemplify "three aspirations which are characteristic of a faith in the future," says Teilhard, and they are: "A passion for the future, a passion for the universal, and a passion for the individual." Though positive in their own right, when misunderstood or imperfectly conprehended, they rain tension and conflict upon the global community. Each ideology attempts to enact these three aspirations of man's faith in the future, only to fail here or there in such a way as to perpetuate human unification.

Democracy, for example, has failed to facilitate the social aspirations of man for full originality and full value because democracy does not respect fully man's personal integrity. Therefore, instead of truly "freeing man" for himself, democracy has simply "emancipated him" from certain politico-social obligations. The dispersion of what Teilhard calls "a false liberalism both intellectual and social" has resulted from the single emancipated cell of society's misguided assumption that it is "free to be its own center." Democracy has achieved only a counterfeit totality, i.e., crowd mentality, because by having given "the people control over progress," it seems to be a true totality of citizen involvement, while in actuality, it adulterates "true universalism" by excluding certain kinds of personal initiatives, values, and potentialities. So the genuinely personal is degraded to the mere individual and the totality of citizen involvement is leveled to that of crowd action, thus "fragmenting and leveling the human mass (p. 52)." Democracy, thereby, has taken genuinely creative human aspirations and has "run the risk of jeopardizing our innate hopes for the future of mankind." Communism, therefore, breaks to the left, while Fascism to the right.

In its beginning formulations, Communism was "magnificently exalted," says Teilhard, as a true "faith in a universal vibrant humanity..." But, says he, because of the Russian neo-Marxists' "temptation for the elite," the latent humanitarian gospel was stifled by a vision of a "totalitarian civilization strongly linked with the cosmic powers of matter," thus leading Teilhard to claim that a more suitable name for present-day communism would be "terrenism," earth as the fundamental basis of reality.

Though the idea was originally sound and derived from the three human aspirations mentioned above, the implementation was unfortunately "defective and deformed" For, says Teilhard, on the one hand, by excessively reacting to Democracy's anarchic liberalism, "Communism soon arrived at the virtual suppression of the individual," whereas on the other hand, "in its unbalanced admiration of the physical powers of the universe, it has systematically excluded from its hopes the possibility of a spiritual metamorphosis of the universe (p. 53)." The phenomenon of man was therefore systematically reduced to the mechanical development of a soulless collectivity," and consequently, bemoans Teilhard, "matter has veiled the spirit. Pseudo-determinism has killed love." The real dangers of Bolshevism, therefore, are twofold: the lack of personalism and the undermining of true universalism.

As with Democracy and Communism, Fascism began as an attempt to address human aspirations for wholeness and unity, but degenerated into rather negative efforts at human manipulation. Reacting against the ideas of the Revolution, Fascism has found much support from those who deny a human future. But even so, it displays an openness to the future by way of its "ambition...to embrace vast entities within its empire." Fascism suffers from a double shortsightedness: not only has it too frequently and apparently deliberately overlooked "the vital human element, the unshakeable material basis" of all human society, but it also and obstinately insists upon building a modern world "in the dimensions of a by-gone age (p. 54)." By this, Teilhard means, Fascism gives preference to "race over mankind," favors a "soul for its own people" while being indifferent to a "soulless world," and looks to the future from the perspective of past historic forms of civilization.

Each in its own way pitiful and pathetic, yet, says Teilhard, Democracy, Communism, and Fascism are all even in their struggles and conflicts "unwittingly converging towards a common conception of the future." For in this "crisis of birth," each one in its own way is "striving to turn toward the light." Indeed, the "world is struggling to achieve itself...essential affinities (characterize them, and) not eternal opposition."

There is now such a dissatisfaction among the peoples of the world with these systems -- their internal logic and their external hostilities -- and a growing expectation that something new is about to emerge as to elicit from those who seek and see the coming higher synthesis a desire to rise and speak. "It is not the fear of perishing," says Teilhard, "which has thrown man into the exploration of nature, the conquest of the atmosphere and the heavens...but the ambition to live (p. 57)." And though this ambition has rightly expressed itself in a science passionately seeking "to unveil the mysteries concealed in matter infinitely great and infinitesimally small," the time is coming (and indeed has now arrived) when scientists will seek ever grander things, viz., "the study of psychic currents and attractions" in what Teilhard calls "a science of spiritual energy."

Teilhard predicts that a scientific community "impelled by the necessity to build the unity of the World (will) end by perceiving that the great object unconsciously pursued by science is nothing else than the discovery of God (p. 58)." Though humanity is always in danger of being absorbed in such secondary matters as philosophical determinism and mechanistic views of society, Christianity is able to speak for man as a free person because it speaks on "behalf of man's conscience" and "maintains the primacy of reflective thought." By belief in "a centered, but still universal consciousness," Christianity can speak of this total convergence both doctrinally and experientially. For, says Teilhard, "the figure of Christ (not only described in a book, but realized concretely in the Christian consciousness) is so far the most perfect approximation to a final and total object toward which the universal human effort can tend without becoming wearied or deformed (p. 59)."

As man looks to his future, he musters within himself a common hope, a shared aspiration, a feeling of corporate confidence and expectation about the destiny of man. And this destiny is wrapped up in the future of earth itself. These feelings of hope and expectation, though they "awaken so belatedly," rise out of and give expression to what Teilhard has called, "the Spirit of Earth." This phrase Teilhard understands to mean "the passionate concern of our common destiny which draws the thinking part of life ever further onward (p. 63)." This Spirit is intrinsic to nature itself, and though it is slow to awaken, it is the firm foundation upon which cosmic evolution is centered. The discovery that "the only truly natural and real human Unity is the Spirit of Earth" is gradually made as human consciousness, still somewhat restricted by circles of "family, country, and race," expands its perimeters.

This growing consciousness of the Spirit of Earth, which is resulting from the increasingly sophisticated discoveries of social and scientific import, is "a conquering passion," says Teilhard, which is sweeping away and transforming earlier premature models of earth. The three-fold nature of this passion is awakening and ordering human consciousness towards the future of earth. The three expressions of this passion are: "The emancipated forces of love, the dormant forces of human unity, and the hesitant forces of research." To understand these three passions is to grasp a "Sense of Earth," and to use these three passions wisely and creatively is to facilitate the cosmic evolution towards God.

"Love," says Teilhard, "is the most universal, formidable and mysterious of cosmic energies (p. 64)." This strange and powerful energy, when viewed within the context of "spiritual evolution," is understood to be the Universal Center's attraction focused upon every conscious particle in the universe. It is a beckon to join the "great union" now beginning to occur in all nature -- and this attraction and beckon, this "primitive and universal psychic energy" called love, charges the whole environment of man, earth, and universe with significance.

The emancipation of this "spiritual quantum" of love too often finds expression in misguided passion, not to enhance the realization of the Spirit of Earth, but to gratify momentary pleasures. The restless search for immediate pleasure bespeaks both this hidden power of love and its misguided use directed towards the immediate and away from the future. "Love is a sacred reserve of energy," says Teilhard, "and the very blood stream of spiritual evolution; that is the first discovery we can make from the sense of Earth (p. 65)."

Not only does the conquering passion of the Spirit of Earth awaken the emancipated forces of love, but also it stirs to consciousness "the dormant forces of human unity." But whereas in love there is present an irresistible attraction, there is competing against human unity what appears to be an "instinctive repulsion" which drives people apart.

Human liberation through unification is stifled by timidity and cowardice on the part of individuals unwilling to face the challenge of unity. The power and strength of the human community to press on in its quest for ever increasing actualization of its potential are derived from the encounter of men with each other, of their bond and power together. Men "suffer and vegetate in isolation," says Teilhard, because they have not sensed this growing power of humanity. "The Sense of Earth is the irresistible presence which will come at the right moment," Teilhard confidently predicts, "to unite them in a common passion (p. 66)."

A third power released in man at the coming of the Spirit of Earth is that of research. "The time has come," announces Teilhard, "to realize that research is the highest human function, embracing the spirit of war and bright with the splendor of religion." The resources now available to man for life process, the powers hidden in the secrets of science, and the growing sense of human unity have outmoded "narrow systems of individual and national division..." We are now in the crisis of birth of a new era. "The age of nations is past," proclaims Teilhard. "The task before us now, if we would not perish, is to shake off our ancient prejudices, and to build the earth (p. 67)." Through research, man continues to apply probing pressure on the "surface of the real," and this probing inquiry constitutes "the supreme gesture of faith in Being." Therefore, Teilard concludes, research is "the highest form of adoration."

The danger inherent in this scenario of optimism is that immature men will think themselves no longer in need of religion. For such men -- pretenders to the title of mature, liberated, scientific moderns -- God is a psychological need whose projection declines with the rise of science and culture. Yet, says Telhard, the very process of scientific research, emancipated love, annd human unity all are in support of a world in need of faith, for the Spirit of Earth increases man's need to "adore." Therefore, "out of universal evolution God emerges in our consciousness as greater and more necessary than ever." The true function of religion for mankind living within the Spirit of Earth is to "sustain and spur on the progress of life." In a true sense, God is continually seeking and finding Himself in the very process of spiritual evolution. And, reasons Teilhard, since everything in the universe beginning with Man occurs in the framework of "personalized being," we must conclude that "the ultimate form of the universal convergence must also possess (in a supreme degree) the quality of a Person."

Before the appearance of Man, the Spirit of Earth felt the attraction for the Center, but was blind and without vital concentrated focus. But with the coming of Man, of human consciousness, the Spirit of Earth is awakening to liberty and to true religion. "Religion," explains Teilhard, "is not an option of a strictly individual intuition, but represents the long unfolding, the collective experience of all mankind, of the existence of God -- God reflecting himself personally on the organized sum of thinking beings, to guarantee a sure result of creation, and to lay down exact laws for man's hesitant activities (p. 71)."

Since the emergence of human self-awareness, i.e., reflective consciousness, the Earth has taken on a new dimension to its evolutionary development -- from **geogenesis** to **biogenesis** to **noogenesis.** "In us," Teilhard points out, "the evolution of the world towards the spirit becomes conscious (p. 75)." The Earth has become conscious through the agency of the human mind, the very mind which the earth through its supportive evolutionary processes has produced. And now, since evolution has become conscious of itself, it will not progress without the concerted effort of man. Evolution "will not happen by itself," warns Teilhard, for now with its increasingly sophisticated mechanism of syntheses, evolution "is constantly acquiring greater freedom," and with increased freedom, an equal capacity for evil and destruction as for good and creativity. In answer to his own question as to "what steps must we take in relation to this forward march?" he answers in five words: **"a great hope, in common (p. 92)."**

The answer is in two parts. First, there must be the presence of a great hope. This great hope must reside in the expectant heart of every believer in the future of the earth. It must swell within the mind of every reflective respondent to the Spirit of Earth. This great hope must rise from a "passionate love of growth, of being," and those who hope must not yield to the moanful wails of "the cowards and skeptics, the pessimists and the unhappy, the weary and the stagnant." This great hope must be held on to tenaciously, and it must be held in common.

The history of human, earthly, cosmic life is decisive on this point -- this great hope must be held in common. "There is only one way which leads upward," says Teilhard, "the one which, through greater organization, leads to greater synthesis and unity (p. 93)." Those who are strong in their faith in the future, who hold this great hope, in common, must not give over to the "pure individualists, the egoists, who expect to grow by excluding or diminishing their brothers -- individually, nationally or racially." The evolutionary process is causing life to rise, and everything that rises must converge -- "Life is moving towards unification." The realization of this great hope held in common will come by means of ever increasing "cohesion and human solidarity."

Due to the emergence of human consciousness, the future of the earth is now in the hands of man, forcing him to answer the question, "How shall we decide?" We cannot simply rely upon a **common science** which "merely brings the geometric point of different intelligences nearer together," and neither can we depend on a **common interest**, regardless of the passion with which it is held, for it "merely brings beings into direct touch, through an impersonal which destroys personality." We do not so much need to bring together our heads and our bodies, says Teilhard, "but our hearts." Our source of unity, the focus of the great hope held in common is mediated through our hearts, but its origin is not man, nor is it derived from Earth. Its origin is above, through, and beneath Man and Earth, giving both Spirit and Personality. "The generating principle of our unification," explains Teilhard, "is not finally to be found in the single contemplation of the same truth or in the single desire awakened by something, but in the single attraction exercised by the same Someone (p. 73)."

The growing encounter with and realization of **Noogenesis,** i.e., the concentration and collective march forward of human thought, leads the believer in the world to give increasing attention and importance to the values of personality and transcendence. We will see the future valuing personality more and more as we accelerate our understanding of the universe as being "on the road of psychic concentration," for this psychic process is synonymous with "a universe which is becoming personalized." And just as we are beginning to grasp the reality of a personalizing universal process, we also can begin to think transcendence is intrinsic in this process. "A last pole of 'cosmic' personalization, if it is to be supremely consistent and unifying," explains Telhard, "can hardly be conceived except as emerging from elements which it super-personalizes by uniting them (p. 97)."

This "mystic transformation," i.e., the cosmic genesis of the spirit, makes the "tangible realities ad laborious conditions" of human progress understandable and precious to the eye of the believer in the future. We are inevitably bound to live in and grow with this reality of cosmic evolution if we are to ever be "super-spiritualized in God." The concourse between man and God is "under-spiritualized in God." The concourse between man and God is understood to be realized in the earth's "opening and flowering upwards" towards God, while God is "rooted and nourished" in the earth. By such a vision, there is no longer possible an antipathy between a personal transcendent God and a universe in evolution, but rather God and earth are entering into a "hierarchic conjunction" for the purpose of lifting the human community into the spiritualizing presence of God. This process Teilhard calls the "spiritual evolution of the universe."

The "solid nucleus" around which tomorrow's unanimity will develop is that of a deep belief in this spiritual evolution -- a "new spirit for a new world." Whether Christians or not, says Teilhard, all those who see and believe that the earth is marching forward compose a unified mass, and though they may "take their stations on opposing wings," as believers in the future, both Christians and humanists must take up the gauntlet and press on towards the future. "In spite of the wave of skepticism which seems to have swept away the hopes (over-simplified and over materialistic) upon which the nineteenth century lived, faith in the future is not dead in our hearts," encourages Teilhard. Indeed, it is this hope alone which promises to save us!

The idea that our human consciousness is slowly but surely awakening to superconsciousness is not only becoming increasingly verified by science, but such an idea seems the only means capable of preparing man for that which is inevitably coming and that for which he is waiting. That is, says Teilhard, "the discovery of a synthetic act of adoration in which are allied and mutually exalted the passionate desire to conquer the world, and the passionate desire to unite ourselves with God...(p. 99)." This is the nature of the **new spirit** which is gradually and assuredly ushering in a **new earth.**

The Spirit of Earth with its imperative "to build the Earth" brings with it the problem and challenge of **human unification.** Of all the demands and pressures of our current times -- individual cares, political, economic, and psychic turmoils -- none are so formidable as is this one. In the not too distant past, it was a common belief that the increasing aggregation of mankind on the earth was little more than a simple demonstration of man's search for a more comfortable life. Today, such a view is pristinely naive, for now we are in a position to better understand through a closer scrutiny of Time and Space those forces which operate under the "veil of human socialization."

These forces are without doubt constantly striving "towards an ever-growing organization of Matter," and, with the decline of Galileo's out-moded and mechanistic description of the Earth as mere spatial motion, we are better able to understand these forces as "the tightening, beyond ourselves and above our heads, of a sort of cosmic vortex, which, after generating each one of us individually, pushes further, through the building of collective units, on its steady course towards a continuous and simultaneous increase of complexity and consciousness (p. 104)." A concomitant of complexity -- biological, psychical, social -- is increasing consciousness (the ever increasing acceleration of the intricately complex relationships of molecules, in the human brain specifically), and beyond consciousness is super-consciousness and ultimate genesis in God.

In view of this evolutionary scheme, Teilhard makes three important observations about the historical and biological position of modern man. First, granted the truth of this scheme of the movement of social totalization as a "drift of cosmic magnitude," then, says Teilhard, "we may be confident that it points the safest (and probably the only) way in which we can engage ourselves if we wish not only to survive, but to live abundantly (supervive)." Second, and because of the "growing compression of expanding Mankind over the closed surface of the Earth," Teilhard contends that "the unifying process in which we are caught is to some extent, not only healing, but **irresistible.**" Third, and in spite of the evolutionary movement and its irresistibility, "it is theoretically possible that if we misuse the liberty which our consciousness has given us relative to our responsibility towards evolution, we could escape the transformation."

"For in order to reach Oneness," argues Teilhard, "Man cannot merely accept this process, but must actively cooperate with the cosmic forces which are striving towards unification (p. 105)." And, therefore, given the dangerous magnitude of this theoretical possibility, "we may say," says Teilhard, "that the bio-economic crisis of Humanity, at the present moment, if reduced to its 'crux,' comes to this single point: namely, **how to maintain in every man a strong interest in the future of man.**"

Teilhard derides those well-meaning but inordinately narrow people who bewail the misuse of the world's resources of thermal energy and food. Even if man could perpetually replenish the heaps of wheat, the mountains of uranium and coal, the oceans of oil, mankind "will starve and decay," warns Teilhard, "unless it guards and feeds the source of its vital passion for more power and more vision." No external pressure will facilitate the preservation of the human species unless Man first and foremost, from deep within, "believes passionately in the future of his evolution (p. 106)."

In the closing pages of BUILDING THE EARTH, Teilhard explores both the objective and the subjective conditions "necessary for the preservation and the growth in humanity of the psychical ardor which is physically indispensable for the completion of its biological development," i.e., the psychological conditions of human unification. In his considerations of the objective conditions for unification, Teilhard suggests that the world must possess both the character of **openness** and a center of **convergency** at the final end of its development. Man is unable to creatively and responsibly carry on his life's work in a world devoid of hope towards the future.

Because of man's reflectivity, he could not survive "the definite prospect of a total disintegration." In view of this image of man, there must be "something fallacious in the widely accepted opinion, based on astronomical and biological evidence, that the future of our species is entirely limited by the physico-chemical evolution of the Earth (p. 108)." In spite of these conclusions, drawn too quickly from unduly shallow evidence, the world cannot be entirely closed if it is to continue to move. Otherwise, says Teilhard, human life would stop due to an absence of internal motivations. The earth is, indeed, open, not only marginally but "centrally, for some kind of triumphant achievement."

Not only is the World open, it is also a centered, i.e., personalizing, world. Man by nature and definition will seek out and respond to only those processes which will "respect and increase, in each human particle, the power it possesses to unify, in an infinitesimal but incommunicable way, the World around itself." No matter the planetary compression, mankind will nurture only those processes which facilitate his broader personalization as opposed to egoistic individualization. We can **accept** the World and its progress towards human unification when seen as having an "upper exit" plus a personalizing center, but "how can we **love** it?" asks Teilhard.

This question brings us to the subjective conditions necessary for human unification. The very drift of universal evolution draws us towards "ultrahumanization," and if we are not only to survive but thrive, we must awaken this passion to full consciousness. Man is presently in a "crisis of puberty," just beginning to sense his innate and explosive powers. Modern man, more so than earlier less scientifically and psychically attuned man, is not only aware of "an open Universe." He is also realizing, because he has suddenly encountered the incredible dimensions and fantastic organicity of the geobiosphere, that "the attraction more distinctly felt for a whole and a oneness (is) no longer conceived or experienced as a dissolving ocean, but as a mighty focus of unification and of completion (p. 110)."

This focus of unification and completion Teilhard understands to have two dimensions -- that of a "clarified sense of the irreversible," and also of a "corrected and generalized sense of the Cosmic or of the Universal..." We are now entering a new age, a new spirit, a new world, wherein these two-fold senses of the Irreversible and the Cosmic are converging in human consciousness such that our primary attention in psychological research will increasingly be focused upon the human experience of the Spirit of Earth. "Ultimately," says Teilhard, "there is no other fuel, no other blood, able to feed (and to humanize at the same time) the giant organism built up by human socialization, but a **new type of faith** in the future of the Species and in a spiritual climaxing of the World (p. 111)." Teilhard concludes with a positive encouragement of man's faith in the future:

Let us not forget that nowhere are the elements of a complete 'evolutive energy' better recognizable and more advanced today than in a well understood Christianity: that is to say, in the flaming perception of a Universe which is neither cold, nor closed -- but which irreversibly converges (Matter and Spirit altogether) on a loving and loveable Center, of intense personality.

BIBLIOGRAPHICAL NOTE

Pierre Teilhard de Chardin (1881-1955)

Biographical Sources

Several biographies of Teilhard's life have appeared in the last decade or so. (Though Teilhard did not write a definitive autobiography, his many volumes of published letters offer some very deep insights into his own perceptions of himself -- who he was, where he was going.) The undisputed authoritative and definitive biography has been written by an acquaintance of Teilhard, Claude Cuenot, TEILHARD DE CHARDIN: A BIOGRAPHICAL STUDY (London: Burns and Oats, 1965), which includes a complete bibliography of Teilhard's works. Another full-length study had been admirably done by Robert Speaght, THE LIFE OF TEILHARD DE CHARDIN (N.Y.: Harper, 1967). Two earlier studies which consider Teilhard's life in the context of his worldview are Nicolas Cortes, PIERRE TEILHARD DE CHARDIN: HIS LIFE AND SPIRIT (N.Y.: Macmillan, 1960), and a joint effort by George Magloire and Hubert Cuypers, PRESENCE DE PIERRE TEILHARD DE CHARDIN: L'HOMME-LA PENSEE (Paris: Ed. Univ., 1961).

Of biographical worth are several books of memoirs by those who knew and worked with Teilhard, such as the notable geologist George Barbour's IN THE FIELD WITH TEILHARD DE CHARDIN (N.Y.:Herder and Herder, 1965); Helmut de Tera's MEMORIES OF TEILHARD DE CHARDIN (N.Y.: Harper and Row, 1964); and Gabriele M. Allegra's CONVERSATIONS WITH TEILHARD DE CHARDIN ON THE PRIMACY OF CHRIST (trans. by B. M. Bonansea, Chicago: Franciscan Herald Press, 1971). An excellent chronicle of Teilhard's career as geologist-paleoanthropologist has been written by Louis Barjon and Pierre Leroy, entitled, LA CARRIERE' SCIENTIFIC DE PIERRE TEILHARD DE CHARDIN (Monaco: Editions de Rocher, 1964). A collection of memorial essays by Teilhard's friends and colleagues has been edited by Neville Braybrooke, entitled TEILHARD DE CHARDIN: PILGRIM OF THE FUTURE (N.Y.: Seabury, 1964). For the beginner, a brief

but informative little biography in the MAKERS OF CONTEMPORARY
THEOLOGY series has been written by Bernard Towers of Jesus
College, Cambridge, entitled, TEILHARD DE CHARDIN (London:
Lutterworth, 1968), which includes a short but helpful bibliography.

Primary Sources

With the exception of numerous scholarly and ofttimes extremely
esoteric journal articles in geology and paleontology, and a few personal
letters, virtually all of Teilhard's writings have been translated into
English. Therefore, only English editions of his works will be mentioned
here. A comprehensive bibliography is out of place here, but some
of his most notable works must be listed. Without doubt, the most
notable work of Teilhard's is, THE PHENOMENON OF MAN (translated
by Bernard Wall, N.Y.: Harper and Row, 1965), with a positive and
critical introduction by Sir Julian Huxley. In this book, Teilhard devel-
opes his understanding of cosmic process and the evolutionary tra-
jectory towards the Omego Point, i.e, God in Christ, by means of
a phenomenological approach to the geological, biological, and intellectual spheres of the earth. Heschel called it "a most extraordinary
book," Karl Stern compares Teilhard to St. Augustine and Pascal concluding that "Teilhard's search will stand out like a flashing beam," for
the future. To read and understand this book is to grasp Teilhard's
vision of the future.

Three more scientific-philosophical works comprise a logical sequel
to THE PHENOMENON OF MAN. They are, THE APPEARANCE
OF MAN (trans. by J. M. Cohen, N.Y.: Harper and Row, 1965), which
is a scholarly inquiry into man's understanding of his own special
evolution, THE VISION OF THE PAST (trans. by J. M. Cohen, N.Y.:
Harper and Row, 1966), another close look at man's primordial history,
those processes which produced him -- body and mind-- and the
implications for the future of man; and, a third major scientific study,
entitled, THE FUTURE OF MAN (trans. by Norman Kenny, N.Y.:
Harper Torchbooks, 1969), which pursues in detail the implications
for the future of man viewed in terms of his evolutionary past. Of
primary interest for Teilhard was the emergence of the human mind,
called "cerebralization," which he felt constituted man's greatest
talent, as it is utilized in the realization of a unified human community,
and facilitates the end of the species in God.

In addition to his scientific-philosophical writings, Teilhard also wrote
what has come to be recognized as a devotional classic, entitled,
THE DIVINE MILIEU (trans. by Bernard Wall, N.Y.: Harper Torchbooks,

1968), which is generally regarded as the devotional companion to his primary scientific study, THE PHENOMENON OF MAN. Here, Teilhard gives vent to a poetic devotion of the deepest spiritual origins in his own priestly life. To read this book is to hear clearly of his faith, his belief in God in Christ, and is the explication of his Christo-centric worldview echoed earlier in its scientific companion. Teilhard the mystic-priest comes to the fore here, as Teilhard the scientist-visionary did in THE PHENOMENON OF MAN.

Jean-Pierre Demoulin has done a great favor for the beginning student of Teilhard's thought by selecting and arranging key passages on a variety of topics from Teilhard's **opus,** entitled, PIERRE TEILHARD DE CHARDIN: LET ME EXPLAIN (trans. by Rene Hague **et. al.,** N.Y.: Harper and Rowe, 1970). A collection of Teilhard's mystical-devotional essays, called by THE CHRISTIAN CENTURY, "...the most mystical and least immediately scientific" of his works, has been published under the title, HYMN OF THE UNIVERSE (N.Y. Harper-Colophon Books, 1965). With an introduction by N. M. Wildiers, this collection contains the most outstanding and widely acclaimed essay, entitled, "The Mass on the World," written by Teilhard in the archeological digs of China away from the facilities of the Church and without the Sacraments.

In response to a request from Mgr. Bruno de Solages in 1934, Teilhard wrote from Peking a little book-essay which has been published under the title, HOW I BELIEVE (N.Y.: Harper and Row, Perennial Library, 1969). He speaks as scientist-priest to such problematic topics as the evolution of his faith -- in world, spirit, immortality, and personal-ity, and of "the Universal Christ and the convergence of Religions." Two collections of Teilhard's brief but provocative essays have been collected under the title, MAN'S PLACE IN NATURE (London: Wm. Collins, 1966), which speaks particularly to the development of the human intellect, i.e., called "noosphere," and our selection for discus-sion, BUILDING THE EARTH (introductory essay on Teilhard by John Kobler, foreward by Max H. Begouen, and trans. by Noel Lindsay and J. L. Caulfield, N.Y.: Avon-Discuss Books, 1969).

Two of the several books in which Teilhard struggled vigorously with the relationship of religion and evolution and of the Church and science, are, CHRISTIANITY AND EVOLUTION (trans. by Rene Hague, N.Y.: Harcourt Brace Jovanovich, 1969), with such notable chapters as "Fall, Redemption, and Geocentrism," "Christology and Evolution," and "The God of Evolution," and SCIENCE AND CHRIST (trans. by Rene Hague, N.Y.: Harper and Row, 1968), with such enlightening subjects as, "Science and Christ or Analysis and Synthesis," "Catholicism and Science," and "Research, Work, and Worship."

Though several volumes of Teilhard's letters have been published, three volumes are relevent for our study: First, a book of letters written during the time Teilhard was serving the medical corps during World War I, entitled, THE MAKING OF A MIND: LETTERS FROM A SOLDIER-PRIEST, 1914-1919 (N.Y.: Harper and Row, 1965); LETTERS FROM A TRAVELLER, 1923-1955 (N.Y.: Harper Torchbook, 1968), which covers the scholarly career of Teilhard including many insights into his spiritual struggles and difficulties with the Catholic Church; and LETTERS TO LEONTINE ZONTA, 1923-1939, with introduction by Robert Garric and Henri de Lubac (N.Y.: Harper and Row, 1968), letters written from China to one of France's most distinguished and brilliant Parisians.

Secondary Sources

For the beginner, no single volume is of more help than that of Alice Valle Knight, THE MEANING OF TEILHARD DE CHARDIN, introduction by Ewert Cousins (Old Greenwich, Ct.: The Devin-Adair Co., 1974). In addition to a brief sketch of Teilhard's life, a basic bibliography of biographical, primary, and secondary sources, there is an excellent succinct treatment of Teilhard's system by way of a topical analysis of key themes. Several French Jesuits are Teilhardian scholars, but the most important studies have been written by Henri de Lubac, S.J., of the University of Lyons, two of which are, TEILHARD DE CHARDIN: THE MAN AND HIS MEANING (trans. by Rene Hague, N.Y.: Hawthorn Books, 1966), a general treatment for the common reader, and THE ETERNAL FEMININE: A STUDY ON THE TEXT OF TEILHARD DE CHARDIN (trans. by Rene Hague, N.Y.: Harper and Row, 1968).

The leading Protestant scholar in France on Teilhard's thought, George Crespy, professor on the faculte de Theologie Protestante at the University of Montpelier, has written a major study of Teilhard's thought as it attempts to conjoin science and religion, entitled, FROM SCIENCE TO THEOLOGY: THE EVOLUTIONARY DESIGN OF TEILHARD DE CHARDIN (trans. by G. H. Shriver, N.Y.: Abindgon, 1968). Along the same theme, Teilhard's major biographer, Claude Cuenot, has written SCIENCE AND FAITH IN TEILHARD DE CHARDIN (trans. by Noel Lindsay, London: Garnstone Press, 1967).

The leading English scholar on Teilhard's thought is Charles E. Raven of Christ Church College, Cambridge, who has written, TEILHARD DE CHARDIN: SCIENTIST AND SEER (N.Y.: Harper and Row, 1962). Holland's Bernard Delfgaauw of the State University of Groningen has written an important study of Teilhard's understanding of evolution and its many implictions for science, man, and the Church, entitled, EVOLUTION: THE THEORY OF TEILHARD DE CHARDIN (introduction by Bernard Towers, trans. by Hubert Hoskins, N.Y.: Harper and Row, 1969). A Jesuit from Fordham University has continued to produce scholarly treatises on Teilhard's thought, Christopher F. Mooney's most significant to date is, TEILHARD DE CHARDIN AND THE MYSTERY OF CHRIST (Garden City, N.Y.: Doubleday Image, 1968), a study drawing upon the importance of hope in the christology of the future.

CHAPTER NINE

"The Meaning-Seeking Animal"

"The problem of meaning in each of its intergrading aspects
is a matter of affirming, or at least recognizing, the
inescapability of ignorance, pain, and injustice on the
human plane while simultaneously denying that these
irrationalities are characteristic of the worls as a whole."

--Clifford Geertz

Introduction

Clifford Geertz is acclaimed today to be one of the most important
theorists in the anthropology of religion. He has approached the
subject matter of religion from that of a humanist seeking to come
to an analytical understanding of the nature of culture as an historically
transmitted pattern of meanings embodied in a complex of symbol-
systems. This approach, i.e., defining anthropology as a science of
meaning-analysis, nurtures the study of culture as a meaning-system.
Religion, too, says Geertz, is a cultural system and necessarily conveys
meaning. Therefore, both culture and religion are meaning-systems
and, we can conclude, both anthropology and theology attempt to
analyze systematically these meaning-systems. The interfacing of
the disciplines of anthropology (systematics of culture) and theology
(systematics of religion) is made possible by the utilization of the
category of "meaning" as a hermeneutical key to the understanding
of both religion and culture as meaning-systems.

§ § §

In an attempt to blaze a humanistic path between positivism and
functionalism, Geertz has put forth what is increasingly being considered the most useful definition of religion to-date in the social sciences.
"The view of man as a symbolizing, conceptualizing, meaning-seeking
animal opens a whole new approach to the analysis of religion," says
Geertz.[1] While attempting to demonstrate the legitimate perimeters
of the social sciences, and especially anthropology, in analyzing religious
phenomena, Geertz conscientiously withholds any challenge to the
methodological credibility of the history and phenomenology of religions
in their pursuit of the essence of religious experience. He has put
forth the following definition: "Religion is (1) a system of symbols

which acts to (2) establish powerful, persuasive, and longlasting moods and motivations in men by (3) formulating conceptions of a general order of existence and (4) clothing these conceptions with such an aura of factuality that (5) the moods and motivations seem uniquely realistic."[2] The design, obviously, is not to construct a definitive definition which exhausts all dimensions of religious phenomena (how absurd such a notion would be!), but rather to construct a realistic and useable definition with intentional limitations and specificity of scope.

Concurring with but not limiting himself to Yinger's definition of religion as a "system of beliefs and practices by means of which a group of people struggles with ultimate problems of human life,"[3] Geertz suggests that a fundamental characteristic of religion is the address to the "problem of meaning" -- meaning suggesting purpose and direction to life and meaninglessness suggesting chaos and pointless existence. "There are at least three points," says Geertz, "where chaos -- a tumult of events which lack not just interpretation but interpretability -- threatens to break in upon man at the limits of his analytic capacities, at the limits of his powers of endurance, and at the limits of his moral insight. Bafflement, suffering, and a sense of intractable ethical pardox are all radical challenges with which any religion, however 'primitive,' which hopes to persist must attempt somehow to cope."[4] Without doing violence to the social scientific perspective of Geertz, we can say that religion constitutes an experientially motivated address to the problem of impending chaos in the existential experience of humankind. Furthermore, we can say that beyond, behind, or under religion's capacity to cope with bafflement, suffering, and inextricable ethical paradox lies the "essence of meaning" to which these expressions in quest of existential meaning are enduring witnesses. This implied extension cannot, of course, be pursued in this study, but I have considered it at length in another place.[5]

Geertz is not oblivious to this possible extension and logical elaboration of his position, nor is he antipathetic to such an endeavor. "The Problem of Meaning in each of its intergrading aspects," continues Geertz, "is a matter of affirming, or at least recognizing, the inescapability of ignorance, pain, and injustice on the human plane while simultaneously denying that these irrationalities are characteristic of the world as a whole."[6] Even an elementary acquaintance with the history of the scientific study of religion is suffucient to establish the qualitative advance Geertz's definition has made, especially as he employs the concept of meaning as an interpretive key. Within his definitional construct Geertz stands head and shoulders above recent efforts to undertand religion by the positivists and functionalists. With his efforts, the way is truly open for an honest dialogue between the social scientists and theologians.   "The existence," Geertz concludes, "of bafflement, pain and moral paradox -- of the Problem of Meaning -- is one of the things that drive men toward belief in gods, devils, spirits, totemic principles, or the spiritual efficacy of cannibalism, but it is not the basis upon which those beliefs rest, but rather their most important field of application."[7]   This "drive toward belief" is conveyed through cultural symbols and bespeaks man's quest for meaning, for an existential meaning which challenges chaos and which pursues order.   "Whatever else religion may be," Geertz says, "it is part an attempt (of an implicit and directly felt rather than explicit and consciously thought-about sort) to conserve the fund of general meanings in terms of which each individual interprets his experience and organizes his conduct..."[8]

MEANING AS HERMENEUTICS

Culture and religion are both symbol-systems which express humankind's quest for meaning.   Therefore, any serious convergence of cultural and religious expressions necessarily centers around the experience of meaning, an experience which is multidimensional and expressed through symbols.[9]   Though culture is historically transmitted as **pattern of meanings** which are embodied in a "complex of symbols," Geertz contends that "meanings can only be 'stored' in symbols," and are not synonymous with the symbols themselves.   Positivists attempt to equate "meanings" with symbols themselves, while functionalists attempt to equate the social "functions" of meaning-symbols with meanings themselves.   Whereas culture and religion are convergent **expressions of meaning,** anthropology and theology are disciplines addressed to the **systematics of meaning,** and as noted above, the analysis of meaning will inevitably involve an analysis of the symbol as meaning-bearer.[10]

Religion as studied by anthropologists involves a two-step operation, according to Geertz: "First, an analysis of the system of meanings embodied in the symbols which make up the religion proper, and second, the relating of these systems to social-structural and psychological processes."[11]   Geertz has consistently demonstrated a receptiveness to the various disciplinary approaches to religious studies, including phenomenology as the study of "religion proper," and has suggested a model for multi-disciplinary complementarity. **Anthropology is an interpretive science** engaged in the **search for meaning** through **a systematic analysis of culture,** i.e., the study of human meanings embodied in symbols. "The concept of culture I espouse," explains Geertz, "and whose utility the essays below (in his collected works) attempt to demonstrate, is essentially a semiotic one."[12] "Analysis," continues Geertz, "is sorting out the structures of significance and determining their ground and import."[13]

In another place, Geertz has said, "The culture concept to which I adhere denotes an historically transmitted pattern of meanings embodied in symbols, a system of inherited conceptions expressed in symbolic forms by means of which men communicate, perpetuate, and develop their knowledge about and attitudes toward life."[14] If culture, then, is the expression of meaning, and anthropology is the analysis of culture, we can say that the fundamental task of anthropology put succinctly is the systematics of meaning. And this systematic analysis, or systematization of meaning, necessitates an analysis of the socio-cultural structures and processes which constitute the framework of meaning. This systems analysis approach implies interpretation, or more correctly, hermeneutics.[15] If culture is the experience and expression of meaning (or rather the context within which and the socio-historical mechanism whereby meaning is both experienced and expressed), then the function of the concept of meaning necessarily is interpretational, or hermeneutical, and in turn, anthropology constitutes the analytical mechanism for identifying and systematizing meaning such as to serve as an effective interpretation of human culture. In other words, **culture is meaning** and **meaning is hermeneutics.**

An essential quality of the anthropological enterprise is its desire for universal application. The cross-cultural perspective is the **sine qua non** of anthropological method. The desired benefit in the employment of anthropological method is the facilitation of what Geertz has called "the enlargement of the universe of human discourse." Anthropology's sensitivity to the vast panorama of human experience exemplified in a substantially built up collection of cross-cultural studies plays a vital role in establishing the discipline's capacity to interpret meaning-systems. In any anthropological analysis of culture patterns, there is an attempt to observe and understand "the degree to which its meaning (i.e., culture's) varies according to the pattern of life by which it is informed."[16] We are confronted with three alternative responses to this anthropological approach to the analysis of culture and religion: (1) To be impressed with the dynamics of cultural diversity while vigorously pursuing the analysis of various culture forms and contents yet foregoing any philosophical speculation as to the implications of such an impression, (2) to be so impressed with cultural diversity that one concludes that life has no "ground" and the only absolute is "relativity," or (3) to be informed by cultural diversity as form-and-content expressions of meaning which are understood to be reflections of **meaning-reality.** The discipline of anthropology, when strictly adhering to its definition as a science for the systematic analysis of socio-cultural phenomena, is bound to the first option -- observation, description, understanding, and interpretation. Nowhere is the discipline forced to adhere either to the second or third options and when it does, it either steps into the circle of positivism (in the second option) or philosophy (in the third option).

We can discount the second option from this discussion as antipathetic to the integrity of anthropology as a social science. (The second option, where tenaciously held to, would result in anthropology's demotion to a mere ideological sect.) From the very outset of our inquiry, we have understood Geertz to be suggesting that anthropology, defined in terms of the first option, when engaged in a dialogue with theology could fruitfully lead to an interfacing of methods suggested in the third option -- a method of religio-cultural analysis. Geertz is clear in his protrayal of the vocation of anthropology appropriate to this point:

> To look at the symbolic dimensions of social action -- art, religion, ideology, science, law, morality, common sense -- is not to turn away from the existential dilemmas of life for some empyrean realm of de-emotionalized forms; it is to plunge into the midst of them. The essential vocation of interpretive anthropology is not to answer our deepest questions, but to make available to us answers that others, guarding other sheep in other valleys, have given, and thus to include them in the consultable record of what man has said.[17]

We need not attempt a resolution here of the age-old philosophical dispute over whether the presence of order is in the world and thus discoverable or whether order is in the mind and thus constructable. The answer to such a problem, though certainly desirable, is not a prerequisite to our observation about man being driven to find/create order-system-category. This drive is suggestive of an imperative in human experience -- no society exists without a conception of order in the world of of system in experience. Within religious community, suggests Geertz, sacred symbols function to synthesize that community's "worldview" (structure of reality -- metaphysics) and its "ethos" (style of life -- values).[18] "The drive to make sense out of experience, to give it form and order," says Geertz, "is evidently as real and as pressing as the more familiar biological needs." This making "sense out of experience" is what we are calling here the systematics of meaning. Though Geertz and another noteworthy social scientist, Peter L. Berger, seem to have resolved for themselves the issue of finding-or-creating order, we need not pass judgement upon that personal preference to concur with this apparent human inperative to order and systematize. "Men are congenitally compelled," suggests Berger, "to impose a meaningful order upon reality."[19] "One fundamental human trait which is of crucial importance in understanding man's religious enterprise," says Berger in another place, "is his propensity for order."[20]

As we have seen, religion and culture are intergrative expressions of meaning. Nevertheless, there is admittedly more to meaning than just its experientially-based expressions. Mankind has always sought to organize his expressions of meaning and no society has ever been devoid of systematizers, as Radin pointed out years ago. "There can be little doubt," Radin observed, "that every group, no matter how small, has, from time immemorial, contained individuals who were constrained by their individual temperaments to occupy themselves with the basic problems of what we customarily term philosophy."[21] And, as with philosophy, so with anthropology, i.e., man's unabated effort to understand and interpret the meaning of life. "Hence," says Geertz in another effort to illustrate the interpretive nature of the science of anthropology, "any scientific approach to the study of symbols (anthropology is essentially a refined science of symbolism) is interpretive in nature. It is a search for meaning which results in an explication of the symbol. In short, anthropological writings are themselves interpretations, and second and third order ones to boot."[22]

In our investigation of the possibilities of interfacing anthropology and theology, Geertz's definition of anthropology as an "interpretive science" has given rise to a characterization of anthropology as the systematic analysis of culture-as-meaning. It can also be suggested that, in an attempt to understand religion-as-meaning, the human propensity for order gives rise to an intellectual interest in the systematic analysis of religion-as-meaning. The social scientific approach to the study of religion, as demonstrated in Geertz, is a systematic analysis of the content and forms of religious and cultural phenomena. Geertz says anthropology does not seek to understand the "basis of belief" but rather belief's manifestations. The task of analyzing and systematizing the "basis of belief" resides squarely in the lap of theologians and philosophers.

Human experience finds expression through the meaning-systems of culture and religion. The analysis of experientially stimulated meaning-expressions and the systematization of this analytic enterprise has occupied our time throughout this deliberation. That we have defined religion and culture in terms of the category of experience must, says Geertz, necessarily inform our definition of anthropology. More precisely, Geertz nurtures an anthropological method which is concentrated upon experiential meaning as the key to understanding both culture and religion. From this we can argue that both religion and culture are meaning and meaning is hermeneutics.

Admittedly, Geertz is not a theologian. he is not even engaging consciously or otherwise in the theological task. As an anthropologist, he is attempting to come to a better understanding of human behavior -- its form, its content, its meaning. In this endeavor, he asserts that the experiential dynamic operative within and reflective through cultural expressions is fundamentally a dynamic of human "meaning." Culture, says Geertz, is a complex interplay of symbols expressing meaning. Therefore, religion as a cultural system is also expressive of meaning, and an expression of Man's search for meaning. This meaning, found in and expressed by religious symbols and cultural systems, is demonstrative of mankind's quest to know and understand his world and his place in it. For theologians interested in the theological interfacing of religion and culture, for social scientists interested in the philosophical importance of "meaning" in socio-cultural analysis, and for religio-phenomenologists interested in the interdisciplinary possibilities between anthropology and philosophy, Geertz's work provides a singularly provocative example of such efforts done well.

NOTES

1. Clifford Geertz, "Ethos, World-View and the Analysis of Sacred Symbols," ANTIOCH REVIEW (Winter, 1957-58), 436. Other major works of Geertz include THE RELIGION OF JAVA (Glencoe: The Free Press, 1960); ISLAM OBSERVED (New Haven: Yale University Press, 1968); THE INTERPRETATION OF CULTURES (New York: Basic Books, 1973); MYTH, SYMBOL, AND CULTURE (New York: W. W. Norton, 1974), edited by Geertz; "Ideology as a Cultural System," in D. Apter (ed.) IDEOLOGY AND DISCONTENT (New York: The Free Press, 1964); "The Impact of the Concept of Culture on the Concept of Man," in J. Platt (ed.) NEW VIEWS OF THE NATURE OF MAN (Chicago: University Press, 1966); "The Growth of Culture and the Evolution of Mind," in J. Scher (ed.), THEORIES OF THE MIND (New York: The Free Press, 1967); "Religion as a cultural System," in M. Banton (ed.), ANTHROPOLOGICAL APPROACHES TO THE STUDY OF RELIGION (London: Tavistock, 1966); and "The Politics of Meaning," in C. Holt (ed.), CULTURE AND POLITICS IN INDONESIA (Ithica: Cornell University Press, 1972).

2. Geertz, "Religion as a Cultural System," p. 5.

3. J. Milton Yinger, THE SCIENTIFIC STUDY OF RELIGION (N.Y.: Macmillan, 1970), p. 7.

4. Geertz, "Religion as a Cultural System," p. 14.

5. See my "Religion and Culture as Meaning Systems: A Dialogue Between Geertz and Tillich," THE JOURNAL OF RELIGION, LVII, 4 (Oct., 1977), 363-375.

6. Geertz, "Religion as a Cultural System," p. 24.

7. **Ibid.**, p. 25.

8. Geertz, "Ethos, World-View and the Analysis of Sacred Symbols," p. 422.

9. **Ibid.**

10. For a consideration of Ernst Cassirer's reference to man as an **animal symbolicum**, see my article, "Theology and Symbol: An Anthropological Approach," JOURNAL OF RELIGIOUS THOUGHT, XXX, 2 (Fall, 1974), 51-61; and also my article, "Religious Myth and Symbol: A Convergence of Philosophy and Anthropology," PHILOSOPHY TODAY, XVIII, 4 (Spring, 1974), 68-84.

11. Geertz, "Religion as a Cultural System," p. 42.

12. Geertz, THE INTERPRETATION OF CULTURES, p. 5.

13. **Ibid.**, p. 9.

14. Geertz, "Religion as a Cultural System," p. 3.

15. A splendid assessment of the current state of philosophical hermeneutics is presented by Richard E. Palmer, HERMENEUTICS: INTERPRETTION THEORY (Evanston, Ill.: Northwestern University Press, 1969), especially his chapter on Heidegger.

16. Geertz, THE INTERPRETATION OF CULTURES, p. 14.

17. **Ibid.**, p. 30.

18. Geertz, "Religion as a Cultural System," p. 23.

19. Peter L. Berger, THE SACRED CANOPY: ELEMENTS OF A SOCIOLOGICAL THEORY OF RELIGION (New York: Anchor, 1969), p. 22.

20. Peter L. Berger, A RUMOR OF ANGELS: MODERN SOCIETY AND THE REDISCOVERY OF THE SACRED (New York: Anchor, 1970), p. 53.

21. Paul Radin, PRIMITIVE MAN AS PHILOSOPHY (New York: Dover, 1957), p. xxi.

22. Geertz, THE INTERPRETATION OF CULTURES, pp. 5, 15.

CHAPTER TEN

"The Systematics of Meaning"

"Culture, creating a universe of meaning, does not create
this universe in the empty space of mere validity. It
creates meaning as the actualization of what is potential
in the bearer of the spirit --- in man."

ᴘᴀᴜʟ   --Paul Tillich

"The view of man as a symbolizing, conceptualizing, meaning-seeking
animal . . . opens a whole new approach . . . to the analysis of religion,"
says Clifford Geertz, of Princeton's Institute of Advanced Studies.[1]
And his philosophy mentor, Susanne Langer, has observed that "the
concept of meaning, in all its varieties, is the dominant philosophical
concept of our time."[2] No stroke of brilliant insight is needed to
notice that the concept of "meaning" has experienced ascendancy
among the philosophers and theologians of our day far more than
among the social scientists, in spite of Weber's emphasis upon the
significance of meaning in sociological analysis -- for example,
when he said that "events are not just there and happen, but they
have a meaning and happen because of that meaning." "No age,"
wrote Heidegger in his KANT AND THE PROBLEM OF METAPHYSICS,
"has known so much, and so many different things, about man as ours.
. . And no age has known less than ours of what man is." The correlation between the ascendancy of the concept of meaning and the growing
experience of bafflement about who and what man is can hardly be
considered accidental. The problem which is explicated by these
two ingredients is man himself. "We are the first epoch," says Scheler,
"in which man has become fully and thoroughly 'problematic' to himself;
in which he no longer knows what he essentially is, but at the same
time also **knows that he does not know.**"[3]

The gaining of public consensus as to the centrality of meaning is
not the issue; rather, the issue facing modern man is the way in which
the problem of meaning is to be articulated and addressed. Heidegger
and Scheler would have meaning considered in terms of being, whereas
Rabbi Heschel would reverse the order: "We have expressed the problem of man in the form of asking: What is being human? . . . Human
being is never sheer being; it is always involved in meaning."[4] When
considering the concept of meaning as a problem, we are in the realm

of the uniquely human experience of reflective inquiry centered upon life as personal and not some abstract metaphysical category. "The dimension of meaning," continues the Rabbi, "is as indigenous to his being human as the dimension of space is to stars and stones . . . Human being is either coming into meaning or betraying it."[5] There is no neutral ground in the experience of meaning. Meaning is experientially personal by definition, and its opposite is equally experiential, that is, meaninglessness. Meaning/meaninglessness are not metaphysical categories but categories of actual human existence. Heschel again speaks to the relationship between being and meaning: "Mental anguish is occasioned more by the experience or fear of **meaningless** being, of meaningless events, than by the mystery of being, the absence of being, or by the fear of non-being. . . . The problem of being and the problem of meaning of being are coexistensive. In regard to man, the first problem refers to what he is in terms of his own existence, human being as it is; the second refers to what man means in terms larger than himself, being in terms of meaning."[6]

After having wandered amid German phenomenology and Jewish philosophy, we must come back to Clifford Geertz's observations about man as a "meaning-seeking animal." Geertz is the latest and by far the most important anthropologist in several generations to employ this concept of meaning in any significantly philosophical fashion in his definitions of religion and culture. "Whatever else religion may be," Geertz says, "it is in part an attempt (of an implicit and directly felt rather than explicit and consciously thought-about sort) to conserve the fund of general meanings in terms of which each individual interprets his experience and organizes his conduct. . . ."[7] Therefore, for a serious anthropological analysis of religious phenomena to occur, Geertz is suggesting that the nature and function of "general meanings" must be analyzed. This is the first major attempt within anthropology to utilize the category of meaning as an integral part of the analysis of religion.[8]

Furthermore, in addition to religion, Geertz is suggesting that a responsible analysis of culture must also cope with the category of meaning. "The culture concept to which I adhere . . . denotes an historically transmitted pattern of meanings embodied in symbols, a system of inherited conceptions expressed in symbolic forms by means of which men communicate, perpetuate, and develop their knowledge about and attitudes toward life."[9] The movement, demonstrated here, beyond definitions of the classical sort which defined culture as "learned human behavior" and "the way of life of a group of people" to a conceptual framework which necessitates dealing in what Langer has called "our stock in trade," that is, sign, symbol, denotation, signification, communication, suggests a shift in emphasis in culture analysis from the "doings" of man to "experiential meaningfulness of tradition (man-in-community)." What else could the term "meaning" as used by Geertz imply but this?[10]

Meaning as human experience is that which constitutes the sine qua non of culture, and so likewise with religion. "Every religion," says the theological anthropologist Robley Edward Whitson, "has come into existence at a point of crisis in the meaning of a community, and remains in existence as long as it continues to make possible the positive confrontation óf succeeding crises."[11] Meaning is not only the core of religion, says Whitson, it constitutes the essential experience of a community of people out of which religion is generated. This relationship between meaning as experience and religion is simultaneously communal and individual in expression. "Religious traditions," he continues, "are always necessarily concerned with the meaning of man not simply as an isolated individual but as a community as well."[12]

The same year that Geertz's article on "Religion as a Cultural System" appeared (1968), a collection of Paul Tillich's essays on his notion of a "theology of culture" came out. The concept of meaning played a vital role in Tillich's treatment of the relationship between religion and culture, and in the following year a collection of his essays entitled WHAT IS RELIGION? appeared, with his most articulate and exhaustive treatment of this idea. Tillich was primarily a philosopher of religion who understood his task to be to delineate a "philosophy of meaning (which could engage) in dialogue with any historical religion . . . (a consideration of man and his) relatedness to the Unconditional in terms of meaning."[13] Having been deeply influenced by the phenomenology of being of Heidegger and the existentialist thought of his day, Tillich combined a quest for a convergence of being and meaning in terms of a category called "meaning-reality," a term incorporating both the experience of meaning and its ground of Unconditionality.

"Meaning," explains Tillich, "is the common characteristic and the ultimate unity of the theoretical and the practical sphere of spirit, of scientific and aesthetic, of legal and social structures. . . Hence, the theory of the structure of meaning-reality, i.e., philosophy, is the theory of the principles of meaning, and its first task is an analysis of meaning itself. . . "[14] As Tillich begins to develop a theory of meaning, he is driven by a complementing relationship between an ontology of being and an anthropology of meaning -- a concern for religion and culture which centers upon the ground of meaning-reality. Yet he is not unaware of the grave and difficult problems awaiting him. He has called the pursuit of the "meaning of meaning a paradoxical enterprise. . . ."[15] In spite of recognized problems, Tillich has suggested three elements which must be considered in any analysis of meaning in religion and culture. First, the interconnectedness of meaning within all separate meanings must center on or face meaninglessness. Second is a recognition of the ultimate meaning of all meaning and thus of every particular meaning. And third is a recognition of the imperative upon every particular meaning to fulfill the unconditioned meaning. There is no meaning which stands alone -- meanings are connected in a total meaning system which legitimizes each separate meaning as they totally reside in the Unconditioned Meaning. "Even the totality of meaning," concludes Tillich, "need not be meaningful, but rather could disappear, like every particular meaning, in the abyss of meaninglessness, if the presupposition of an unconditioned meaningfulness were not alive in every act of meaning."[16] For Tillich, to raise the question or possibility of meaninglessness is to have already posited meaning.

Under the philosophical influence of Susan Langer, Geertz has brought the term "meaning" fully into anthropological parlance with a definition of culture as "an historically transmitted pattern of meanings embodied in symbols. . . ."[17] Geertz is not a radical behaviorist who readily correlates the Skinnerian rat box with human social interaction, nor is he a mushy humanist who quickly moves from a token deference to data to a moralistic agenda. As with Tillich and his monumental effort to articulate the complexity of meaning-reality, Geertz is striving throughout his writings upon religion and culture to express the dynamics of human expresions in ritual and symbol as demonstrative of man's quest for meaning.

Possessed with a passion to come to terms with meaning as a fundamental ingredient in human culture, Geertz sets out to articulate the distinction between culture and social system -- the confusion of the two having been a continual plague for social scientific theorizing, especially in the analysis of social and cultural change -- by noting that culture is "an ordered system of meaning and of symbol, in terms of which social interaction takes place, . . ." whereas a social system is "a pattern of social interaction itself. . . ."[18] This distinction gave him more precision in his utilization of the variables within each of the two categories of culture and social system and also led to a deeper understanding of the coextensive elements between them -- what Geertz later came to call the "socio-cultural." In view of this elucidated distinction, Geertz proceeded to characterize "culture (as) the fabric of meaning in terms of which human beings interpret their experience and guide their action," whereas "social structure is the form that action takes, the actually existing network of social relations."[19] If Geertz is indeed a functionalist, as my innuendo ventured to suggest earlier, he is a revisionist-functionalist, for he seeks to come to grips with dimensions of human culture, particularly of meaning, which except for Weber have too frequently gone unattended by traditional functionalism.[20]

In spite of the broadened and deepened scope of the concept of meaning developed and employed by Geertz, the absence in his usage of the ontological and existential dimensions of meaning leaves his treatment of culture as an expression of meaning incomplete. The philosophy of Tillich has added another dimension to our consideration of culture as an expression of meaning, and, though the implications are somewhat differently drawn from Geertz as over against Tillich, these implications do not appear to be inexorably antipathetic. The moods are different and must be held in creative tension:

(Tillich:) Culture, creating a universe of meaning, does not create this universe in the empty space of mere validity. It creates meaning as the actualization of what is potential in the bearer of the spirit -- in man. . .[21]

(Geertz:) The concept of culture I espouse . . . is essentially a semiotic one. Believing, with Max Weber, that man is an animal suspended in webs of significance he himself has spun, I take culture to be those webs, and the analysis of it to be therefore not an experiential science in search of law but an interpretive one in search of meaning . . . Meaning, that elusive and ill-defined pseudoentity we were once more than content to leave philosophers and literary critics to fumble with, has now come back into the heart of our discipline.[22]

Attempting to demonstrate the perimeters within which and the methodology by which anthropology can legitimately analyze religious phenomena while simultaneously holding back any inclination to question the credibility of theology and phenomenology in their pursuit of the essence of religious experience, Geertz has put forth the following definition: "Religion is (1) a system of symbols which acts to (2) establish powerful, persuasive, and long-lasting moods and motivations in men by (3) formulating conceptions of a general order of existence and (4) clothing these conceptions with such an aura of factuality that (5) the moods and motivations seem uniquely realistic."[23] The design obviously is not to construct a definitive definition which can exhaust all the dimensions of religious phenomena -- how absurd such a notion would be! -- but, rather, to construct a definition with intentional limitation and specificity of scope.

Concurring with but not limiting himself to Yinger's definition of religion as a "system of beliefs and practices by means of which a group of people struggles with . . . ultimate problems of human life,"[24] Geertz suggests that a fundamental characteristic (might we say "function"?) of religion is the address to the "problem of meaning" -- meaning suggesting either purpose and direction to life or meaninglessness, chaos, pointless existence. "There are at least three points," says Geertz, "where chaos -- a tumult of events which lack not just interpretation but interpretability -- threatens to break in upon man at the limits of his analytic capacities, at the limits of his powers of endurance, and at the limits of his moral insight. Bafflement, suffering, and a sense of intractable ethical paradox are all . . . radical challenges . . . with which any religion, however 'primitive,' which hopes to persist must attempt somehow to cope."[25] Without doing violence to the social scientific perspective of Geertz, we can say that religion functions as an experientially motivated address to the problem of impending chaos in man's existential life.

Geertz is not oblivious to possible extensions and logical elaborations of his position by theologians, nor is he antipathetic to such endeavors. "The Problem of Meaning in each of its integrating aspects . . .," continues Geertz, "is a matter of affirming, or at least recognizing, the inescapability of ignorance, pain, and injustice on the human plane while simultaneously denying that these irrationalities are characteristic of the world as a whole."[26] Even an elementary acquaintance with the history of the scientific study of culture and religion is sufficient to establish the qualitative advance of Geertz's treatment of religion and culture over efforts of the past.

Within his definitional construct, Geertz stands head and shoulders above all past efforts by the positivists and functionalists to understand religion and culture -- the way is truly open for an honest dialogue between the social scientist, philosopher, and theologian. "The existence," Geertz concludes, "of bafflement, pain and moral paradox -- of the Problem of Meaning -- is one of the things that drive men toward belief in gods, devils, spirits, totemic principles, or the spiritual efficacy of cannibalism . . . but it is not the basis upon which those beliefs rests, but rather their most important field of application."[27]

These expressions characteristic of religion are conveyed through cultural symbols all of which bespeak the problem of meaning -- an existential meaning -- for man against chaos and in pursuit of order.

Geertz lays no claim of competency in speaking to the "basis upon which belief rests," having intentionally focused his attention upon the problem of meaning as it is expressed in and through the cultural symbol systems of man. He has, however, set the stage from an anthropological perspective for a dialogue with theology, and Tillich has written the prologue.

Tillich, a philosopher of religion and self-labeled "theologian of culture," has not restricted his observational analysis as Geertz has done to the cultural manifestations; he feels a professional imperative not only to speak of religion and culture as meaning systems but to plumb for their ground of being, what he calls their "meaning-reality." J. Luther Adams, a theologian of note and commentator on Tillich, has observed that for Tillich man "strives to fulfill the possibilities of being," "being" characterized as a "meaning-reality that is inescapable and which is never subject to manipulation with impunity. . ."[28] The Heideggerian influence in the form of a phenomenology of being is obvious in Tillich's system. But he is not bound by this influence but develops it to serve the theological task in addressing being as "meaning-reality," the "unconditionality of meaning" which is present in every act of the human spirit -- theoretical, aesthetic, practical.[29] "Meaning," continues Adams in his preface to a collection of Tillich's essays, "is three fold" for Tillich. "It is an awareness of a universal interconnection of meaning, an awareness of the ultimate meaningfulness of the interconnection of meaning, and an awareness of a demand to fulfill, to be obedient to, the ultimate, unconditional meaning-reality."[30] Though not inevitably antipathetic to Geertz, Tillich has necessarily gone beyond the realms of anthropological analysis of religion and culture as meaning systems. In order to take account of that out of which existential meaning derives, the nature of meaning must be sought in terms larger than man to avoid the tautological problem mentioned earlier and to avoid the existentialist trap of a human monologue, propounded by Nietzsche and Sartre, analyzed by Berger, and attacked by Heschel and Buber.

Meaning-reality, to use Tillich's term for the existential/essential duality of meaning as being, cannot be expressed in the raw but, rather, must be experientially expressed through religiocultural media, that is symbol systems.[31] "Meaning finds expression in forms that have a particular content," explains Adams, "but form and content as such do not require more than relatedness to the interconnection of meaning. . . The more fundamental element . . . Tillich called the **Import** of meaning (reminiscent of Hegel's **Lectures on Aesthetics**)."[32]   Tillich, as I noted earlier, is profoundly sensitive to the cultural milieu within which all human experience occurs, for existential meaning is transmitted through the forms and contents of culture.[33]   The form and content of culture characterize the manner in which meaning is portrayed, expressed, established; but form and content are only indirectly focused upon or responsible to the Unconditional which constitutes the source of all existential meaning. That quality of meaning which distinguishes between culture and religion Tilich has called "import."[34] "Authentic religion," then, can be described as "directedness toward this import, directedness toward the Unconditional."

With such a distinction between religion and culture based on the dimensions of the experience of meaning, we have set before us an analytic structure which allows of both the cultural and the theological. **Culture** is the expression of meaning through its forms and contents directly addresssed to Essential Meaning, the Unconditional; whereas **religion** is the expression of meaning, imbedded in cultural forms and contents, intentionally focused upon the Essential, the Unconditional, as this ground or meaning-reality is conveyed through its import of meaning. Cultural meanings are single directed through its forms and contents; religion, on the other hand, is double directed because of its awareness of not only form and content but also import; that is, it is directed toward "the conditioned forms of meaning and their interrelations" and also toward "the unconditional meaning-reality which is the ground of the import."

For Tillich, neither religion nor culture can be spoken of in the absence of the other, for they both convey meaning, granted the difference in direction and level of intensity. "Culture is defined," therefore, "as lacking this double-directedness (toward form and import): it is oriented only to the conditioned forms and the interrelation of meaning. Yet culture is substantially, if not intentionally, religious, for every meaning is supported by the unconditioned meaning-reality." This notion that culture is substantially religious, due to the necessary reliance of its existential meaning upon the unconditioned meaning-reality, is central to Tillich's thought and, from the point of view of an anthropological analysis of culture as meaning, offers a most positive possibility for dialogue.

Geertz and Tillich have made use of the concept of meaning in a manner heretofore ignored or overlooked, and, though Geertz has contributed substantially to this growing climate of dialogue, Tillich has taken the first bold step. "In abbreviation," says Tillich in another place, "religion is the substance of culture, culture is the form of religion."[35] Whereas religion is **intentionally** focused upon the Unconditional by means of the import of meaning, culture is **substantially** focused upon the forms and contents of meaning and thus is religious by substance but not by design. For Tillich, the direction that expressions of meaning take becomes the distinguishing determinant between religion and culture, succinctly recorded in this quote from Tillich: "If consciousness is directed toward the particular forms of meaning and their unity, we have to do with **culture**, if it is directed toward the unconditioned meaning, toward the import of meaning, we have **religion**. **Religion is directedness toward the Unconditional, and Culture is directedness toward the conditioned forms and their unity.**"[36]

Obviously Tillich has begun with a task in mind which oversteps the aspirations as well as the methodology of anthropology. And yet we cannot readily dismiss this effort as simply ideology. If Tillich has defined culture in terms agreeable to good anthropology (of the kind demonstrated by Geertz) and if his definition of religion, though not substantially in anthropological terminology, is not antipathetic to anthropological method, then there is a beginning point for dialogue. I have been suggesting here that that dialogic point is the concept of meaning in religion and culture. A quote from Tillich provides encouragement:

> **In the cultural act, therefore, the religious is substantial; in the religious act the cultural is formal.** Culture is the sum total of all spiritual acts directed toward the fulfillment of particular forms of meaning and their unity. Religion is the sum total of all spiritual acts directed toward grasping the unconditioned import of meaning through the fulfillment of the unity of meaning. . . The field in which culture and religion meet is the common directedness toward the unity of meaning. . . In the sphere of knowledge culture is directedness toward the conditioned forms of existence and their unity. Religion in the sphere of knowledge is directedness toward the unconditionally existing as the ground and abyss of all particular claims and their unity.[37]

In terms of the dynamics of meaning operative in culture, as in religion, there is an "actualization" process at work which goes beyond a "creation" suggested by Sartre: "Culture, creating a universe of meaning," explains Tillich, "does not create this universe in the empty space of mere validity. It creates meaning as the actualization of what is potential in the bearer. . ."[38]

Culture and religion are expressions of meaning, the former through existential form and content, the latter through essential import. Therefore a convergence of cultural and religious expressions occurs with the concept of meaning -- a multidimensional experience communicated through symbols.[39] Whereas culture and religion are convergent **expressions of meaning**, anthropology and theology must be understood to be disciplines addressed to the **systematics of meaning**, and, as suggested above, the analysis of meaning will inevitably involve an analysis of the symbol as meaning bearer.

Religion as studied by anthropology involves a two-step operation, according to Geertz: "First an analysis of the system of meanings embodied in the symbols which make up the religion proper, and second, the relating of these systems to social-structure and psychological processes."[40] Earlier I considered Geertz's treatment of social and cultural as mutually related, neither being intrinsically dominant. Geertz has attempted to demonstrate receptiveness to the various disciplinary approaches to religious studies, even phenomenology as the study of "religion proper," by way of suggesting a model of multidisciplinary complementarity.

Anthropology is an interpretive science engaged in the search for meaning through a systematic analysis of culture -- that is, man's meaning embodied in symbols.[41] This precision of directedness upon culture implies a scientific method of categorizing. "Analysis," says Geertz, "is sorting out the structures of significance . . . and determining their ground and import."[42] If culture is the expression of meaning and anthropology is the analysis of culture, then we can say that the fundamental task of anthropology put succinctly is the **systematics of meaning** -- meaning here being the existential meaning of form and content. On the vocation of anthropology, Geertz has said, "To look at the symbolic dimensions of social action -- art, religion, ideology, science, law, morality, common sense -- is not to turn away from the existential dilemmas of life for some empyrean realm of de-emotionalized forms; it is to plunge into the midst of them. The essential vocation of interpretive anthropology is not to answer our deepest questions, but to make available to us answers that others, guarding other sheep in other valleys, have given, and thus to include them in the consultable record of what man has said."[43]

I need not attempt a resolution here of the age-old philosophical dispute over whether the presence of order is **in the world** and thus discoverable or **in the mind** and thus constructable. The answer to such a problem, though desirable, is not a prerequisite to my observation about man being driven to find/create order-system-category. This drive is suggesstive of an **imperative** in human experience -- no society exists without a conception of order in the world, of system in experience. "The drive to make sense out of experience," says Geertz, "to give it form and order, is evidently as real and as pressing as the more familiar biological needs." This making "sense out of experience" is what I am calling the "systematics of meaning." Though Geertz and Berger -- as in the latter's statement, "Men are congenitally compelled to impose a meaningful order upon reality" -- seem to have resolved for themselves the issue of finding/creating order, it is not necessary to pass judgment upon that personal preference to concur in this apparent imperative of ordering or systematizing.[44]

Though religion and culture are complementing expressions of meaning, the former through import and the latter through form and content, there is more to meaning than just its experientially based expression. Men seek to organize their expressions of meaning -- no society is devoid of these systematizers.[45] And, as has been seen in Geertz's explanation of anthropology as an "interpretive science" which gave rise to our characterization of anthropology as the systematic analysis of culture as meaning —— we now see that the human propensity for order has given rise to an **intellectual enterprise engaged in the systematic analysis of religion as meaning, viz., theology.** The social scientific approach to the study of religion, as demonstrated in Geertz, is the systematic **analysis of the content and form** of religious and cultural phenomena, whereas the theological approach to the study of religion, as demonstrated in Tillich, is a systematic **analysis of the import** of religious and cultural phenomena. Whereas Geertz says anthropology does not seek to understand the "basis of belief" **but, rather,** belief's manifestations, Tillich says that theology is an address to the basis of belief **by means of** belief's religious and cultural manifestations.

Tillich's view of theological method and its relationship to cultural analysis is helpful here. "Philosophy and theology (address) the question of being," Tillich says, explaining that "philosophy deals with the structure of being in itself; theology deals with the meaning of being for us."[46] Heidegger's influence upon the ontological structure of Tillich's philosophy of religion has already been mentioned. More important for my interest is Tillich's characterization of theology as concerned with the "meaning of being for us." Through Tillich's method of "correlation,"[47] the ontological question of "being in itself" is answered from the existential question of the "meaning of being for us," that is, philosophy asking and theology answering.

Theology is man's systematic attempt to answer the ontological question. Theology is generated out of actual human experience, and therefore, says Tillich, "the theological . . . is a universal application of theological questioning to all cultural values." The universality of the theological method is for Tillich a logical conclusion drawn from the universal questioning of man about "being" and its "meaning" for him.[48] "We have assigned to theology," continues Tillich, "the task of finding a systematic form of expression for a concrete religious standpoint."[49] The concreteness of the religious experience constitutes the fundamental focus of theology in order for the logical abstraction of systematic analysis (theology) to speak to the human condition.

As anthropology begins with the experience in culture of existential meanings expressed in culture's form and content, likewise theology begins with the experience in religion of Essential Meaning expressed in religion's import. "Our whole development of this theme," says Tillich, "has taken culture and its forms as a starting point and has shown how culture as such receives a religious quality when substance or import flow into form, and how it finally produces a specifically religious-cultural sphere in order to preserve and heighten that religious quality."[50] Theology is system; it is universally applicable; it is focused upon the ultimate concern of men as they express themselves in religious and cultural meaning systems.

Tillich wrote extensively regarding the development of theological method, especially developed in the first volume of his SYSTEMATIC THEOLOGY. There were two formal criteria characteristic of his theological system. First, "The object of theology is what concerns us ultimately. Only those propositions are theological which deal with their object in so far as it can become a matter of ultimate concern for us." Second, "Our ultimate concern is that which determines our being or not-being. Only those statements are theological which deal with their object in so far as it can become a matter of being or not-being for us."[51] These two criteria must characterize every theological method and sytem if those methods and systems are understood to be the systematization of religious experience. However, it is the theology of culture within the systematic theology of Tillich which is of special importance here, for "the theology of culture," explains Tillich, "is the attempt to analyze the theology behind all cultural expression, to discover the ultimate concern. . ."[52] No cultural expression is without a religious substance, though the cultural expression's intention is not religious as such. A theology of culture is a systematic analysis of the substance of culture in an attempt to discover culture's religious core.

A theology of culture must be established upon a well-developed systematics wherein the method of correlation, that is, philosophy asking and theology answering, informs the theologizing process, according to Tillich. But also a genuine theology of culture must be substantially informed by and in touch with its own culture -- its moods and styles. Tillich, a noteworthy historian of art and a recognized art critic, understood the interplay in his own life of the theological and the aesthetic. As Tillich's theology of culture grows out of his systematic theology, so his systematics is necessarily centered in actual human experiences of meaning which seek for religious and cultural expressions. "The sources of systematic theology," says Tillich, "can be sources only for one who participates in them, that is, through experience."[53]

A theology of culture seeks the theological infrastructure of all cultural expressions, and wherever culture expresses itself a theology of culture has its task laid out. "The task of a theology culture," explains Tillich, "is to follow up . . . all the spheres and creations of culture and to give it (the theology behind culture) expression."[54] Of course theology has its own agenda and is not designed to encroach upon other methods of cultural analysis but, rather, seeks to sit among the various methods with equal privilege **as method.** Theology's approach is "not from the standpoint of form," according to Tillich, for "that would be the task of the branch of cultural science concerned -- but taking the import or substance as its starting point, as theology of culture and not as cultural systematization." The distinction is crucial -- that between cultural systematization of form (anthropology) and the systematic analysis of import (theology) -- for otherwise the very discipline which I wish to engage in dialogue would be engaged in competitive interpretations.

Unless the distinctions are held constant between form/content and import, such efforts will fail. Tillich is attempting to develop a theology which would be considered "a normative science of religion" -- my term explains this as the "systematics of religion." The concrete religious experiences embedded in all great cultural phenomena," suggests Tillich, "must be brought into relief and a mode of expression found for them." And therefore what is needed and what Tillich labored for was, in addition to a normative science of religion focused upon the universal religious experiences of men embedded in cultural phenomena, a theological method which could stand beside systematic theology "in the same way that a psychological and a sociological method, etc., exists alongside systematic psychology."

My effort has been to demonstrate the possibility of a positive dialogue between anthropology and theology. Beginning with a current definition of culture as "pattern of meanings" (Geertz) and religion as "man's encounter with the meaning of being" (Tillich), I have worked through these meaning systems to their systematic analysis, defining anthropology as the "systematics of culture" and theology as the "systematics of religion." The possibilities for mutual interaction between anthropology and theology are thereby made clearer.

NOTES

1. Clifford Geertz, "Ethos, World-View and the Analysis of Sacred Symbols," ANTIOCH REVIEW (Winter 1957-58), p. 436.

2. Susanne K. Langer, PHILOSOPHICAL SKETCHES (New York: Mentor Books, 1964), p. 54.

3. As quoted in M. Buber, BETWEEN MAN AND MAN (New York: Macmillan Co., 1968), p. 182.

4. Abraham J. Heschel, WHO IS MAN? (Stanford, Calif: Stanford University Press, 1968), p. 50.

5. **Ibid.**, p. 51. For an in-depth treatment of this point, see John Morgan, "From Human Being to Being Human: The Creative Dialectic in Rabbi Heschel's Thought," AMERICAN BENEDICTINE REVIEW XXVIII, 4 (Dec., 1977): 413-430.

6. Heschel, p. 52.

7. Geertz, p. 422.

8. ENCYCLOPEDIA BRITANNICA, 11th ed., s.v. "anthropology." (The article is by B. Malinowski.)

9. Clifford Geertz, "Religion as a Cultural System," in ANTHROPO-LOGICAL APPROACHES TO THE STUDY OF RELIGION, ed. Michael Banton (London: Tavistock Publications, 1968), p. 3.

10. See Conrad Phillip Kottak, ANTHROPOLOGY: THE EXPLORA-TION OF HUMAN DIVERSITY (New York: Random House, 1974), p. 492: "culture -- behavior patterns acquired by humans as members of society"; and William A. Haviland, ANTHROPOLOGY (New York: Holt, Rinehart & Winston, 1974), p. 8: "When we speak of culture, we refer to man's learned behavior. . . Culture is the way of life of an entire people."

11. Robley E. Whitson, THE COMING CONVERGENCE IN WORLD RELIGIONS (New York: Newman Press, 1971), p. 8.

12. **Ibid**, p. 10.

13. Paul Tillich, WHAT IS RELIGION? (New York: Harper Torchbooks, 1969), pp. 22, 19.

14. **Ibid.**, p. 57.

15. Paul Tillich, SYSTEMATIC THEOLOGY (Chicago: University of Chicago Press, 1967), 3:304.

16. Tillich, WHAT IS RELIGION? p. 57.

17. Geertz, "Religion as a Cultural System," p. 3. For a critique of current models, see John Morgan, "Religious Myth and Symbol: A Convergence of Philosophy and Anthropology," PHILOSOPHY TODAY 18, no. 4 (Spring 1974): 68-84.

18. Clifford Geertz, "Ritual and Social Change: A Javanese Example," in READER IN COMPARATIVE RELIGION: AN ANTHROPOLOGICAL APPROACH, ed. William A. Lessa and Evon Z. Vogt, 2nd ed. (New York: Harper & Row), p. 549.

19. **Ibid.**

20. **Ibid.**, p. 548.

21. Tillich, SYSTEMATIC THEOLOGY, 3:84.

22. Clifford Geertz, THE INTERPRETATION OF CULTURES: SELECTED ESSAYS (New York: Basic Books, 1973), pp. 5, 29.

23. Geertz, "Religion as a Cultural System," p. 4.

24. J. Milton Yinger, THE SCIENTIFIC STUDY OF RELIGION (New York: Macmillan Co., 1970), p. 7.

25. Geertz, "Religion as a Cultural System," p. 4.

26. **Ibid.**, p. 24.

27. **Ibid.**, p. 25.

28. In his preface to Tillich, WHAT IS RELIGION?, p. 19.

29. **Ibid.**, p. 58.

30. **Ibid.**, p. 19.

31. See John Morgan, "Theology and Symbol: An Anthropological Approach" JOURNAL OF RELIGIOUS THOUGHT 30, no. 2 (Fall-Winter 1973-74): 51-61.

32. Tillich, WHAT IS RELIGION? p. 20.

33. **Ibid.**, p. 50.

34. **Ibid.**

35. Paul Tillich, THEOLOGY OF CULTURE (Oxford: Oxford University Press, 1968), p. 42.

36. Tillich, WHAT IS RELIGION? p. 59; emphasis added.

37. **Ibid.**, pp. 60, 66; emphasis added.

38. Tillich, SYSTEMATIC THEOLOGY, 3:84.

39. Paul Tillich, "The Religious Symbol," DAEDALUS: JOURNAL OF THE AMERICAN ACADEMY OF ARTS AND SCIENCE, 87, no. 3(Summer 1958): 3-21.

40. Geertz, "Religion as a Cultural System," p. 42.

41. Geertz, THE INTERPRETATION OF CULTURES, pp. 5, 29.

42. **Ibid.**, p. 9.

43. **Ibid.**, p. 30.

44. Peter Berger, THE SACRED CANOPY: ELEMENTS OF A SOCIO-LOGICAL THEORY OF RELIGION (New York: Anchor Books, 1970), p. 46.

45. See Paul Radin, PRIMITIVE MAN AS PHILOSOPHER (New York: Dover Pbulications, 1957).

46. Tillich, SYSTEMATIC THEOLOGY, 1:22.

47. George F. Thomas, "The Method and Structure of Tillich's Theology," in THE THEOLOGY OF PAUL TILLICH, ed. Charles W. Kegley and Robert W. Bretall (New York: Macmillan Co., 1961).

48. Tillich, SYSTEMATIC THEOLOGY, 1:42.

49. Tillich, WHAT IS RELIGION? p. 165.

50. Tillich, THEOLOGY OF CULTURE, p. 29.

51. Tillich, SYSTEMATIC THEOLOGY, 1:12, 14.

52. Ibid., 1:39.

53. Ibid.

54. Tillich, WHAT IS RELIGION? p. 164.

CHAPTER ELEVEN

"Personal Meaning as Therapy"

"Ultimately, man should not ask what the meaning of his
life is, but rather must recognize that it is he who is asked.
And he can only answer to life by answering for his own life.
Thus, logotherapy sees in responsibleness the very essence
of human existence."

--Victor Frankl

Introduction

In recent years, Victor E. Frankl, the Viennese psychiatrist who is
the founder of what has come to be known as the Third Viennese
School of Psychology -- Freud and Adler constituting the founders
of the other two schools -- has emerged as the leading proponent
in psychotherapeutic circles of the centrality of the experience of
"meaning" in mental health. The goal of human life, argues Frankl,
is to find meaning and order in the world for "me" personally and
"us" collectively -- both as an individual and a social sense of purpose
and orderliness of the inner and outer environment. This chapter
attempts to identify -- within the framework of the Jewish mystical
tradition the sources and origins of Frankl's scientific constructs
in psychotherapy, and their manifestations in psychoreligious thera-
peutics.

§ § §

The story is told of Schopenhauer who, customarily strolling through
a Berlin park during the wee hours of the morning in shabby clothes
and sockless feet, was halted and questioned by a conscientious police
officer: "Who are you? Where are you going?" To this our German
philosopher answered true to form, "I wish to God I knew!" As this
little story graphically illustrates, in modern times, life has become
a struggle for reason and purpose. The sense of alienation which
results in a concomitant sense of loss in personal identity and a growing
recognition of an all-pervading estrangement from self and others,
from personhood and neighborhood, from ego-identity and social identity, is so common that the feeling has become a cultural given. "The
concept of meaning in all of its varieties," explains Suzanne Langer,
"is the dominant philosophical concept of our time."[1]

Modern-day fixation upon and bafflement over our individual meaning
-- "the meaning of meaning" -- is evidenced in every serious effort
at the construction of a workable politic and social ethic. And yet,
explains Heidegger, "no age has known so much, and so many different
things, about man as ours. . . And no age has known less than ours
of what man is."[2] In fact, in view of the current agitation over the
need for an effective definition of man, we can honestly say we are
in a "crisis of meaning." "We are the first epoch," corroborates Max
Scheler, "in which man has become fully and thoroughly 'problematic'
to himself; in which he no longer knows what he essentially is, but
at the same time also knows that he does not know."[3]

In recent years, Victor E. Frankl,[4] the Viennese psychiatrist who
is the founder of what has come to be known as the Third Viennese
School of Psychology (Freud and Adler constituting the founders of
the other two schools), has emerged as the leading proponent in psychotherapeutic circles of the centrality of the experience of "meaning"
in mental health.[5] Frankl dismissed Freud's inordinate emphasis
upon the pleasure principle -- what we might call here for the sake
of symmetry the "will-to-pleasure" -- contending that pleasure for
mankind only has significance and purpose within the context of the
individual's own grasp of life's meaning for himself, i.e, life as personal.
Furthermore, Frankl denigrates the Second Viennese School of Psychology, i.e., Alfred Adler and his notion of mankind's "will-to-power,"
by arguing that personal power in the face of suffering and in the
absence of personal meaning has no visible function within the personality.[6]

The goal of human life, argues Frankl, is to find meaning and order
in the world for me personally and us collectively -- both an individual
and a social sense of purpose and orderliness of the inner and outer
environment. Resulting from his heart-rending wartime Nazi concentration camp experience -- where death and dying, suffering and
inhumanity reign supreme -- Frankl became convinced of the **sui
generus** nature of the **will-to-meaning**, what he later developed
as logotherapy.[7] Amidst suffering and inhumanity, alienation and
tragedy, he encountered the ever-impending onslaught of meaninglessness. Within the walls of an earthly man-made hell, an inhumanity
which had taken his mother and wife and which threatened his own
existence, he faced, as stark nakedness of body and soul the possible
absence of any meaning to life. And yet, though the temptation for
inmates to throw themselves upon the high voltage wires encircling
the camp was ever present and often intense -- indeed, even claiming
the lives of some -- nevertheless, most did not succumb to what

Dostoyevski has diabolically referred to as the ultimate expression of human freedom, namely, suicide. In spite of unbelievable suffering and persecutions, most persons sought out and held on tenaciously to a sense of personal meaning in a world reduced to stark nothingness.

Sitting in the filth and hideousness of humanly contrived persecutions, where pain was omnipresent and death commonplace, Frankl's thoughts rose above his situation as he reflected upon the plight of others and himself. Later in life he writes:

> I remember my dilemma in the concentration camp when faced with a man and a woman who were close to suicide; both had told me they expected nothing more of life. I asked both my fellow prisoners whether the question was really what we expected from life. Was it not, rather, what life was expecting from us? I suggested that life was awaiting something from them.[8]

As a result of Frankl's concentration camp experience at Auschwitz,[9] he discovered that man's greatest need is not the will-to-pleasure nor the will-to-power, but rather the will-to-meaning, the need to find meaning for one's own life. Through this discovery, and his utilization of this need in therapeutic situations, he developed what today is acclaimed as a major school in psychotherapeutic psychology. By helping prisoners then and patients later remember their past lives -- their joys, sorrows, sacrifices, and blessings -- he emphasized the "meaningfulness" of their lives as already lived.[10] During moments of apparent helplessness and meaninglessness, these recollections serve therapeutically to stabilize and reinforce the meaningfulness and purposefulness of life. He emphasizes not only the recollected past, but calls attention to the existential meaningfulness of suffering and tragedy in life as testimonies to human courage and dignity.[11]

In logotherapy, Frankl differentiates meaning and values.[12] Values are socially held meanings whereas meaning as the **sine qua non** of life is a unique experience and possession of every single individual in every moment of one's own life. Frankl contended that this will-to-meaning -- as Freud argued for "pleasure" and Adler for "power" -- pervades every theatrical stage as well as every secret recess of one's personal life. Meaning, he pointed out, can be found in any situation within which man finds himself.[13] The concentration camp inmates could live only if they could make sense -- will-to-meaning -- out of their apparently senseless suffering. the fact that they lived and survived to tell of it speaks empirically enough of this will-to-meaning. Where human life exists, there meaning is to be found.

The surprising feature about Frankl's psychotherapeutic formulations is that throughout he consistently makes inferential comments about the religious dynamic operative in his theory while constantly omitting any specific reference to its fundamentally Jewish character.[14] Especially does he consistently fail to refer, even at most commodious opportunities, to the presence of a strong element of Hassidic teachings, i.e., the teachings of the rabbis who rose up in the eighteenth century in Eastern Europe in reaction against an overemphasis on talmudic learning . . . and radical mystical Messianism.

If David Bakan is even "tacitly" correct in his attribution of religious motives to Sigmund Freud's psychological formulations, we cannot be far wrong in the identification of major Jewish principles in Viktor Frankl's psychology.[15] As Freud utilized, whether consciously or not, the conceptual frameworks of the Hassidic book of mysticism, the ZOHAR, so Frankl unquestionably used the philosophical teachings of the Hassidic rabbis in his considerations of life's meaning.[16] And yet, nowhere does Frankl face frankly the legitimate philosophical question: "From whence cometh this meaning?" Is it a human contrivance a la Sartre, or a discovery? Frankl answers with the letter, but gives no satisfactory explanation as to the origin or source of this meaning. However, appropriate to this discussion, Fackenheim supplies us with a genuinely religious view of the Jewish perception of this query. "In the eyes of Judaism, whatever meaning life acquires derives from this encounter: The Divine accepts and confirms the human in the moment of meeting. But the meaning conferred upon human life by the Divine-human encounter cannot be understood in terms of some finite purpose, supposedly more ultimate than the meeting itself. For what could be more ultimate than the Presence of God?"[17] For the religiously sensitive Jewish thinker, humankind cannot simply be satisfied with the discovery of meaning for oneself, but must plumb deeper for the source of all meaning. The Presence of God, Buber has explained, is an "**inexpressible** confirmaton of meaning. . . The question of the meaning of life is no longer there (when God is Present). But were it there, it would not have to be answered."[18] And though we would not wish to fault Frankl prematurely or unfairly, we might have legitimately expected from a Vienese Jewish psychiatrist an expression of his sensibility to the philosophical problem implied in his psychology and the source of his philosophical perspective in addressing these problems.

The therapeutic efficacy of his logotherapy is not open to question, but accountability for its rational basis must be pondered. As we have considered at length in another place, man is not simply satisfied

with an ontological answer to his existential query, "Who am I?,"
but is also in pursuit of the source of the answer when it comes. That
Frankl is indebted to Jewish teaching is without question. "What
Frankl calls 'logotherapy' and the 'will to meaning,'" explains Rubenstein, himself a rather critical Jewish philosopher of the post-
Auschwitzian variety, "is not unlike the striving for an ordered, meaningful cosmos on the part of the rabbinic teachers in their own
times."[19] Rubenstein believes that for Frankl, this reaching back
into his own religious heritage, i.e, the Hassidic tradition of Viennese
Judaism, constituted the only basis upon which Frankl could ever
hope to decipher the ultimate meaning of the concentration camp
horrors. Without such a legacy, Frankl and his fellow inmates would
have surely succumbed. "Only by resorting to the age-old Jewish
interpretation of misfortune," explains Rubenstein, "could he (Frankl)
maintain his sanity." That Rubenstein is correct in his conclusion
is certainly open to discussion (and in my personal opinion he is doing
little more than attempting to disparage Frankl's religious faith in
the wake of his own faithlessness), but that Frankl's psychology and
Jewish philosophy are intertwined is indisputable.

In Frankl's logotherapy, not only is man portrayed as being in possession
of a **sense of meaningfulness** but also of a personal **sense of indebtedness**.[20] Not only is life charged with meaning, this meaning implies
responsibility. Life is for me meaningful and I, therefore, must respond.
Life provides an arena within which I must discover meaning, and
this discovery places **upon me** "an expectation **of me**." Let us quote
Frankl exactly on this point:

Ultimately, man should not ask what the meaning of his life
is, but rather must recognize that it is **he** who is asked. In a
word, each man is questioned by life; and he can only answer
to life by **answering for** his own life; to life he can only respond
by being responsible. Thus, logotherapy sees in responsibleness
the very essence of human existence.

To demonstrate the fundamentally religious character of Frankl's
psychology, we need only look to the writings of Rabbi Abraham Joshua
Heschel who is without question America's most respected Jewish philosopher in this century. "The dimension of meaning," says Heschel,
"is as indigenous to his (mankind's) being human as the dimension
of space is to stars and stones. . . Human being is either coming into
meaning or betraying it."[21] In other words, all of human life is a
struggle to maintain a relationship to meaning, and though this relationship ebbs and flows with the rise and fall of our conscientious quest

for meaning or our recalcitrant niggardliness in seeking it, humankind is continually confronted with the choice of meaning or meaninglessness. Heschel explains further:

Imbedded in the mind is a certainty that the state of existence and the state of meaning stand in relation to each other, that life is accessible in terms of meaning. The **will to meaning** and the certainty of the legitimacy of our striving to ascertain it are as intrinsically human as the will to live and the certainty of being alive.

Heschel offers a clarification to the ambiguity suggested in Frankl's perception of meaning -- from where does it derive and who is it for. If meaning is derived from within man himself and is strictly for his personal aggrandizement, we are not better off than Freud's pleasure seeker, Adler's power seeker, or Sartre's pathetic drunkard who chose freely not to serve his fellowman. "What we are in search of," clarifies Heschel, "is not meaning for me, an idea to satisfy my conscience, but rather a meaning transcending me, ultimate relevance for human being."

Let us consider more carefully this dual sense of meaning and indebtedness, alluded to in Frankl and explicated in Heschel. What Frankl faced in the camps and what we all confront at various moments in our lives is the immanence of despair, of forlornness, of a sense of nothingness. "There is not a soul on this earth," contends Heschel, "which has not realized that life is dismal if not mirrored in something which is lasting,"[22] Heschel's criticism of Sartre and Nietzsche is precisely here -- mankind is not his own measure. "Tell man he is an end within himself," warns Heschel, "and his answer will be despair." Humankind is not his own judge and jury and "despair is not (his) last word," says Heschel, nor is "hiddenness God's last act."[23]

Though Heschel agrees that humankind is fundamentally "a being in search of meaning," unlike Frankl, he is not satisfied in stopping at that observation. To the biblical mind, explains Heschel, "man is not only a creature who is constantly in search of himself, but also **a creature God is constantly in search of.**" Furthermore, says Heschel, "man is a creature in search of meaning because there is meaning in search of him, because there is God's beseeching question, 'Where art thou?'" Here is the juncture at which Frankl's psychology must give way to Jewish philosophy -- where meaning no longer is an "a priori" given but an explanation of a prior relationship which exists between God and humankind. The meaning of human life derives from the source of all meaning -- "God is in need of man... To Jewish religion, history is determined by this covenant."[24] Religion, culminating in its Jewish expression, consists of God's question -"Where art though?," and in humankind's answer -- "I was afraid" (Gen. 3:9-10). Human meaning derives from God, and God is searching for humankind.

It is with this insight that we can come to a better understanding of our own nature. Meaning does not derive from humankind for humankind does not produce meaning, neither can he look to himself in hopes of understanding the nature of meaning. "Man is man," explains Heschel, "not because of what he has in common with the earth, but **because of what he has in common with God.**"[25] Humankind cannot endow the sky with stars, neither can he bestow upon mankind inalienable rights. Equality of humankind is not due to humankind's own ingenuity, but rather "is due to **God's love and commitment to all men . . .** (For) wherever you see a trace of man, there is the presence of God."

Only when humankind lifts its sights above frivolities, inhumanity and selfishness, can we hope to sense the meaning of life, for, says Heschel, "the destiny of man is to be a partner of God."[26] This, says he, is the "main event in Israel's history," namely, "God's search for man." It is here we see the underpinnings of Frankl's psychology of the will-to-meaning. Humankind seeks meaning because meaning seeks humankind. "This," says Heschel, "is the central message of the biblical prophets. God is involved in the life of man." And with this, we can move from our extrapolation of the "sense of meaning" expressed in Frankl to his emphasis upon a concomitant "sense of indebtedness" resulting from this discovery of meaning. Frankl's appeal to a sense of meaning while caring for his fellow inmates rested upon his capacity to elicit from them a sense of life's expectations of them. Legitimate human existence consists not in my expectations of life but of life's rightful expectations from me.

But where do these "rightful expectations" come from? Surely not from within humankind, for just as certainly as humankind cannot generate its own meaning, neither can one hope to generate one's own expectations. Furthermore, under such circumstances, how could any ethic exist? When humankind becomes his own source of expectations, his animality, not his humanity, comes to the fore. We need only witness again the rise of Nazi Germany! To unravel this quandry, from "whence cometh" humankind's meaning, Heschel explains that "man is man because something is at stake in his existence." This sense of a requiredness of human existence is fundamental to all of humankind, and in religious life, humankind moves beyond isolation from self and into communion with God.

"Religion," explains Heschel, "begins with a consciousness that something is asked of us." With this, we must read Frankl's therapeutic efforts at making individuals aware of life's expectations of them as essentially religious and pastoral in nature. Not that we would denigrate this function. Quite the contrary, to the extent that Frankl's logotherapy functions to put individuals in touch with life's meaning and its implied debt, we can rightfully expect from him an allegiance to his own religious heritage. "The essence of Judaism," says Heschel, "is the awareness of the reciprocity of God and man, of man's **togetherness** with Him...(for) Man does not exist apart from God. The human is the borderline of the divine."

In Judaism, explains Heschel, "man cannot think of himself as human without being conscious of his indebtedness."[27] For Heschel as for Shopenhauer's police officer, human consciousness rises to religious sensibilities at the point of asking "Who am I?" and "What am I to do?" "Religious consciousness," says Heschel, "is to be characterized by two features -- it must be a consciousness of an **ultimate commitment** and it must be a consciousness of **ultimate reciprocity.**" The "is-ness" of human meaning is complimented by the "oughtness" of religious consciousness. And the ultimate expression of this consciousness in the "Jewish religion . . . is the **awareness of God's interest in man,** the awareness of a **covenant,** of a reciprocity that lies on Him as well as on us."

In this scenario, we have seen how Frankl's logotherapy, which is a psychotherapeutic method employed to assist individuals in getting in touch with life's meaning and its implied indebtedness, draws heavily from the Hassidic tradition within Jewish philosophy most recently extrapolated in the writings of Abraham Joshua Heschel. We have not attempted to indict Frankl as a deceptive and conniving rabbinic teacher in psychiatric garb, but rather have attempted to vindicate Frankl's logotherapy from the appearance of being devoid of philosophical underpinnings. Further, we have attempted to indicate that his psychology is quite defensible both in terms of existential psychology and Jewish philosophy. Frankl's theory, it seems, is thus rendered stronger thanks to its identifiable philosophical defensibility witnessed in Heschel's recitation of the Hassidic tradition.

NOTES

1. Suzanne K. Langer, PHILOSOPHICAL SKETCHES (New York: Mentor, 1964), p. 54.

2. Martin Heidegger, KANT AND THE PROBLEMS OF METAPHYSICS (Bloomington, Ind.: Indiana University Press, 1962), p. xxi.

3. As quoted in Martin Buber, BETWEEN MAN AND MAN (New York: Macmillan, 1968), p. 182.

4. Frankl's major works include, FROM DEATH CAMP TO EXISTEN-TIALISM (Boston: Press, 1959); THE DOCTOR AND THE SOUL: AN INTRODUCTION TO LOGOTHERAPY (New York: Alfred A. Knopf, 1963), and MAN'S SEARCH FOR MEANING (New York: Washington Square Press, 1964).

5. See Viktor E. Frankl, "Psychiatry and Man's Quest for Meaning," JOURNAL OF RELIGION AND HEALTH, Vol. 1, pp. 93-103, 1962.

6. Viktor E. Frankl, "Logotherapy and the Challenge of Suffering," PASTORAL PSYCHOLOGY, Vol. 13, pp. 25-28, 1962.

7. Viktor E. Frankl, "The Will to Meaning," THE JOURNAL OF PASTORAL CARE, Vol. 12, pp. 82-88, 1958.

8. Frankl, MAN'S SEARCH FOR MEANING, pp. 12-13.

9. See Frankl, Pt. One, "Experience in a Concentration Camp," in MAN'S SEARCH FOR MEANING, pp. 3f.

10. Viktor E. Frankl, "Group Psychotherapeutic Experiences in a Concentration Camp," GROUP PSYCHOTHERAPY, Vol. 7, pp. 81-90, 1954.

11. VIktor E. Frankl, "Logotherapy and the Challenge of Suffering," REVIEW OF EXISTENTIAL PSYCHOLOGY AN PSYCHIATRY, Vol. 1, pp. 3-7, 1961.

12. Viktor E. Frankl, "Dynamics, Existence and Values," JOURNAL OF EXISTENTIAL PSYCHIATRY, Vol. 2, pp. 5-16, 1961.

13. Viktor E. Frankl, "Logos and Existence in Psychotherapy," AMERICAN JOURNAL OF PSYCHOTHERAPY, Vol. 7, pp. 8-15, 1953.

14. Cf. Viktor E. Frankl, "The Spiritual Dimension in existential Analysis and Logotherapy," JOURNAL OF INDIVIDUAL PSYCHOLOGY, Vol. 15, pp. 157-165, 1957, and Viktor E. Frankl, "Religion and Existential Psychotherapy," THE GORDON REVIEW, Vol. 6, pp. 2-10, 1961.

15. Frankl, MAN'S SEARCH FOR MEANING, pp. 154, 156, 157.

16. Frankl has paid at least passing attention to the philosophical implications of his work, but not specifically to Hassidism. Cf. Viktor E. Frankl. "Psychotherapy and Philosophy," PHILOSOPHY TODAY, Vol. 5, pp. 59-64, 1961. Chapter Two.

17. Emil L. Fackenheim. QUEST FOR PAST AND FUTURE: ESSAYS IN JEWISH THEOLOGY. (Boston: Beacon Press, 1970), p. 245.

18. Martin Buber, I AND THOU (New York: Charles Scribner's, 1958), p. 110.

19. Richard L. Rubenstein, THE RELIGIOUS IMAGINATION: A STUDY IN PSYCHOANALYSIS AND JEWISH PHILOSOPHY (Boston: Beacon, 1968), p. 177.

20. Frankl, MAN'S SEARCH FOR MEANING, p. 13: "...The question was really what...life was expecting from us."

21. Abraham J. Heschel, WHO IS MAN? (Stanford: University Press, 1968), p. 50.

22. Abraham J. Heschel, MAN IS NOT ALONE: A PHILOSOPHY OF RELIGION (New York: Farrar, Straus, and Giroux, 1972), p. 198.

23. Abraham J. Heschel, ISRAEL: AN ECHO OF ETERNITY (New York: Farrar, Straus, and Giroux, 1974), p. 135.

24. Heschel, BETWEEN GOD AND MAN, p. 51.

25. Heschel, THE INSECURITY OF FREEDOM, p. 152.

26. Abraham J. Heschel, GOD IN SEARCH OF MAN: A PHILOSOPHY OF JUDAISM (New York: Harper Torchbooks, 1966), p. 312.

27. Abraham J. Heschel, A PASSION FOR TRUTH (New York: Farrar, Straus, and Giroux, 1974), p. 259.

CHAPTER TWELVE

"Meaning as Hermeneutics"

"Man manifests his humanity by interpreting, not just reacting,
to his environment, i.e., human experience seeking understanding."

--John H. Morgan

Everywhere in the modern world is evidenced an almost frantic compulsion for mankind to understand himself and his world. Whether we peruse the latest works in literature, art, or music, the result is the same -- man seeks to understand himself and his world. But such understanding, though sought after with passionate drive, continually eludes him. "The tragedy of modern man," says Abraham J. Heschel in venturing to explain modern man's present crisis, "is that he thinks alone."[1] In mankind's frantic search to understand himself and his relationship to his world, he is continually baffled and mystified by his persisting inability to define himself in terms relevant to his humanity, terms larger than himself with power to draw him forward into the future. "The greatest challenge of modern man," explains Teilhard de Chardin, "is to establish an abiding faith in the future."[2]

But in order for such a faith to emerge, man must not only have a singularly personal sense of "What am I?" but also a universally social sense of "Who is Man?" "No age," observes Martin Heidegger, "has known so much, and so many different things, about man as ours . . . And no age has known less than ours of what man is."[3] The problem, as Heidegger so clearly sees, is not a deficiency in technical knowledge, in scientific information, in bio-medical and psycho-social aptitude and insight, but rather the problem is deeper and lies behind all this burgeoning of knowledge, information, aptitudes and insights. The problem is not man's intellect. The problem is man himself. Knowledge of the world seems not to be a problem, but the understanding of man himself and his relationship to the world does. "We are the first epoch," observes Scheler, "in which man has become fully and thoroughly 'problematic' to himself; in which he no longer knows what he essentially is, but at the same time also knows that he does not know."[4]

Of course, to know that one does not know is one step towards addressing the problem responsibly. What seems to be absent from the modern experience is any context or frame of reference within which or from which judgements can be made with conviction, a position from which lives can be lived with authenticity. "The most poignant problem of modern life," explains the Nobel Prize winning biologist, René Dubos, "is probably man's feeling that life has lost significance."[5] The gradual encroachment of pervasive relativism -- a sense that nothing is any more or less significant than anything else -- seems to have successfully assaulted man's own self-image more so than any of his particular ideologies or industries.

And when man looks to his ancient past for some root from which to regain strength to carry on and renew his vigor to reaffirm the humanness of his being, mankind falters. What was perceived in days of resoluteness to be way-markers in man's self-understanding degenerates in days of self-doubt to little more than halfhearted speculations. When men are strong, they revere their past for the power they see there; but when men falter, their past too loses power. As the French philosopher Ernst Cassirer has so painfully pointed out, "Nowhere in Plato's Socratic dialogues do we find a direct solution to the problem, 'What is man?' There is only an indirect answer, 'Man is declared to be that creature who is constantly in search of himself -- a creature who in every moment of his existence must examine and scrutinize the conditions of his existence."[6]

From Plato we learn little about the nature of man, but we learn much about that which makes man human. His humanity is manifest in his drive to know, as Aristotle once said centuries ago -- to know who he is and what his relationship is to the world. "He is a being in search of meaning," says Heschel.[7] And, in seeking to know himself, man defines his world. He interprets his world in terms of his own humanity. Throughout history, the human crisis has always centered around man's search for himself, for meaning, a meaning which derives from his propensity to interpret. By virtue of interpreting his world, man creates a history and history for man is the record of his discovery of meaning for himself within his world. And meaning in turn becomes the mechanism whereby he continues to understand and interpret. A discussion of this development, of man interpreting himself and his world in terms of relationship-as-meaning, is the purpose of this chapter.

In man's quest to understand himself, in his drive to examine and scrutinize the conditions of his existence, to come to grips with his world, he must inevitably engage in interpretation. Man confronts a world of reality which, if he is to survive and thrive, he must interpret. The issue is not so much whether he creates or discovers order and purpose in this world of reality as the fact that this reality (real or imagined) compels him to encounter it and interpret it. "I believe," says Marias, "that the universe is covered by a patina of interpretations."[8] Of course, what is not being implied here is that reality is merely interpretation. On the contrary, "reality is something that makes me make interpretation (emphasis mine)." The human quality of the lived experience in the world of reality is fundamentally interpretational. Man never achieves a sense of this reality without interpretation.

Amidst this frantic compulsion to know himself by means of interpreting the world, we must not suppose that mankind's humanity has any analogue in the physical environment from which to draw comparisons. Whereas the physical -- the sub-human environment -- can be described in terms of its objective properties, Cassirer argues cogently that "man may be described and defined only in terms of his consciousness."[9] That which so decisively differentiates the physical world of reality from the human world of reality is consciousness -- man's reflective selfawareness. Teilhard de Chardin once observed that the difference between man and animal is that the latter "knows" but the former "knows that he knows."[10]

Though man, as animal, encounters his world as a physical reality, man, as human, encounters his world as an interpreted reality. This distinctiveness of man vis a´ vis animal is not merely a quantitative leap in breadth of worlds perceived but is a qualitative leap in depth of worlds experienced. Whereas man like other animals employs receptor and effector systems of bio-physical adaptation to his physical environment, man alone has discovered the symbolic system as explained so cogently by Cassirer. "This new acquisition transforms the whole of human life. . . As compared with other animals man lives not merely in a broad reality; he lives, so to speak, in a new dimension of reality."[11] We might wish to call this a *milieu symbolicum.*

This new dimension of reality is a discovery of man resulting from his drive to interpret his world -- an encounter with the symbolic dimension of a world perceived in abstract space. This is the distinctive character of the human species, that it has developed the capacity for abstraction through symbolization, and in abstracting from the physical world man interprets the symbolic world known only to himself. And herein lies the humanness of man's encounter with and desire to understand this new dimension, this symbolic world, which demands not only a subject-object encounter but an interpretation. "Wherever a man dreams or raves," explains Paul Ricouer, "another man arises to give an interpretation; what was already discourse, even if incoherent, is brought into coherent discourse by hermeneutics."[12] Man manifests his humanity by interpreting, not just reacting, to his environment, i.e., human experience seeking understanding.

As noted earlier, the modern crisis is one of meaning, man's inability to interpret his world in a manner that makes what he does, thinks, and dreams make a difference. "The concept of meaning," suggests Langer, "in all its varieties, is the dominant philosophical concept of our time."[13] The dominance of the concept of meaning bespeaks the pervasiveness of the perceived problem. Man is in search of his own humanity, or in the words of Carl Gustav Jung, "Modern man in search of a soul."[14]

And in the search, and within the new dimension of symbol, mankind requires a sense of orderliness, predictability, rationality, understandability. "Men are congenitally compelled," says Berger, "to impose a meaningful order upon reality."[15] Though I had rather say man is compelled to discover a meaningful order within reality, nevertheless, the "propensity for order . . . (is) one fundamental human trait" which is crucial in understanding the compulsions of man to interpret as meaningful the world of reality.[16]

It should be evident by now that what I mean by understanding through interpretation is not simply an explanation of the world as man encounters it. Long ago, Dilthey cleared up the matter of distinguishing between explanation and understanding as applied to human awareness. "We explain," says he, "by means of purely intellectual processes, but we understand by means of the combined activities of all the mental powers in apprehending . . . We explain nature; **man we must understand** (emphasis mine)."[17] We can say then that in the act of understanding man's nature, he comes through mental effort to comprehend living human experience.

Only man can have a crisis of meaning for only man can understand his world by interpreting the complexities of his encounter with the new dimension of the milieu symbolicum. And in this dimension, which he interprets, man confronts the historical nature of his being in the world. Richard Palmer has aided us along this train of thought by focusing not only upon Cassirer's description of man as animal symbolicum but also and concomitantly upon man's compulsion to interpret this new dimension of reality. "In hermeneutical theory," Palmer explains, "man is seen as dependent on constant interpretation of the past, and thus it could almost be said that man is the 'hermeneutical animal,' who understands himself in terms of interpreting a heritage and shared world bequeathed him from the past, a heritage constantly present and active in all his actions and decision."[18] It is in historical consciousness that man becomes fully human and necessarily confronts his own humanness. By virtue of his compulsion to interpret a world he desires to understand, a world limited to his capacity for abstraction through symbolization, man discovers history. "In historicality," says Palmer, "modern hermeneutics finds its theoretical foundations."

In man's desire to know, to come not merely to an explanation of his physical environment but to understand by interpretation the symbolic dimension of reality which he alone has discovered, he is inevitably confronted with the emergence of an historical conscious-ness. "Man has no nature," Ortega y Gassett once said, "what he has is history."[19] Certainly what has been presented here thus far is not so much an attempt to definitionally circumscribe human nature so much as to characterize the human propensity as interpretational, as hermeneutical, as symbolic, as historical. Heidegger said in defer-ence to Dilthey's enamoration of history tnat "historical understanding is something belonging to the way of being man." We have seen that with the emergence of consciousness, i.e., reflective self-awareness, within the human species a new dimension of reality has been discov-ered, understood, and interpreted such that an historical sensibility is an inevitable and indispensable correlary of man's own humanity.

With the overall effort here being to illustrate that man's propensity to interpret his world rests upon a sense of history as meaning and meaning as hermeneutic, Palmer has said that the "hermeneutical experience is intrinsically historical."[20] As noted earlier, man, unlike animanls, confronts an objective world which he encounters not only with his receptor and effector sensory systems, but unlike other ani-mals, man also and distinguishingly encounters an abstract world of symbols. "Ideal reconstruction," says Cassirer, "not empirical observation, is the first step in historical knowledge . . . (For) the historian finds at the very beginning of his research a symbolic uni-verse."[21] It is at the level of historical knowledge that man so uniquely distinguishes himself above the physical world of animal life. Man interprets what he encounters, and his interpretation is historical in character.

The interpretation of man's place in the world is essentially an expression of his perception of relationships -- relationships as embodying a sense of life's meaning. "The component parts of what comprises our view of the progression of our life *(Auschauung es Lebensverlaufes),*" explains Dilthey, "are all contained together in living itself."[22] Whereas Kantians would have us believe that this inner temporality or historicality is superimposed from a priori mental categories, we would rather argue for their being intrinsic to man's world as Dilthey and Heidegger, among others, have so convincingly argued in modern times. The point is crucial to all hermeneutics and is determinative for our work. "Experience," explains Palmer, "is intrinsically temporal (historical), and therefore understanding of experience must also be in commensurately temporal categories of thought."[23]

Historicality *(Geschichtlichkeit)* as used here is formed by Dilthey's thesis that "what man is only history can tell him."[24] The term usually carries a dual meaning, discussed at length by Otto Friedrich Bollnow, viz., first, the fact that man understands himself not so much through introspection as through the objectification of life, and second, that man's nature is not a fixed essence but rather that in the phrase of Dilthey, man is a "not-yet-determined animal" *(noch nicht festgestellte tier).*[25] Thus we see the inevitability of man's interpretation of his world, being an expression of his quest for meaning, as an historical event. The intrinsic temporality of understanding itself, as Heidegger has argued, is in seeing the world always in terms of past, present, and future. This we are calling the historicality of understanding. "Meaning," Palmer has suggested, "always stands in a horizontal context . . . (such that) the concept of 'historicality' . . . comes to refer not only to man's dependence on history for his self-understanding and self-interpretation but also to the inseparability of history and the intrinsic temporality of all understanding."[26]

Understanding, Heidegger has taught us, is the basis for all interpretation. By understanding, he would have us mean man's power to grasp his own "possibilities for being" within the "lifeworld of our existence." As Heidegger sees it, understanding operates within a set of already interpreted relationships, or in Heidegger's own term, "relational whole *(Bewandtnisganzheit).*" And, whereas understanding implies interpreted relationships, Dilthey has earlier suggested that meaningfulness is always a matter of reference to a "context of relationships *(Strukturzusammenhaug).*"

Historicality as man's interpretation of his perceived relationships to the world and himself manifests itself in terms of man's quest for meaning. Human history, we are suggesting, is the result of man's interpretation of perceived relationships -- his grasp through interpretation of meaning. "History," Cassirer once said, "is relationship (meaning) understood." Meaning is the essence of history as history is the essence of human interpretation of the new dimension of reality, a dimension which can only be understood and interpreted in terms of the experiential category of meaning. "Meaning," continues Palmer, "is the name given to different kinds of relationships."[27]

It is at this juncture, of history as meaning, that man's nature so poignantly manifests and reveals itself. In grasping his world -- relation as meaning -- man grasps himself, the maker of history and the discoverer of its meaning. "History is not knowledge of external facts or events," explains Cassirer, "it is a form of self-knowledge . . .In history man constantly returns to himself."[28] As man is compelled to interpret his newly discovered milieu symbolicum, he comes to know that the meaning of history is most exactly the history of meaning, a process whereby man interpreting his abstract environment comes to a working definition of himself. "Not through introspection," says Dilthey, "but only through history do we come to know ourselves."[29]

It is through interpretation, says Heidegger, that man confronts the problem and meaning of his own being. "The logos of a phenomenology of Dasein," explains Heidegger, "has the character of *hermeneuein* (to interpret), through which are made known to Dasein the structure of his own being and the authentic meaning of being given in his (preconscious) understanding of being."[30] Therefore, we might convincingly argue that historicality -- man's consciousness of the sequential nature of interpretation -- constitutes the proper milieu for man's self-understanding. And, therefore, in interpretation, i.e., hermeneutics, we find man's best efforts at finding, within the context of the quest for meaning, the nature of his own being. "Phenomenology of Dasein," continues Heidegger, "is hermeneutics in the original sense of the words, which designates the business of interpretation . . . Hermeneutics," concludes Heidegger, "has become interpretation of the being of Dasein."

If Heidegger has strengthened our belief that hermeneutics as interpretation of the being of Dasein is indispensable in man's quest for self-knowledge, then Dilthey has vindicated our sense of history as meaning, the experiential framework of relationships embodying the meaningfulness of existence interpreted and understood. In experience itself, temporality is expressed in the context of relationship, for experience is not a static phenomenon, but rather, "in its unity of meaning it (experience) tends to reach out and encompass both recollection of the past and anticipation of the future in the total context of 'meaning'."[31]

Historical consciousness emerged within the context of a human experience of compulsion to interpret the abstracted relationships and realities of a symbolic world. And in the emergence of this consciousness, man came to realize that the meaning of this compulsion, the meaning of this history was really the history of man's meaning. "Meaning," Dilthey pointed out, "cannot be imagined . . . (rather) the past and the future form a structural unity with the presentness of all experience, and perception in the present is interpreted."[32] In this discovery of meaning, revealed in history to man through his drive to know his world by interpreting it, man has discovered the means by which life can be grasped. The meaning of the being of Dasein is within human reach.

The crisis of modern man we have been saying is a crisis of meaning. Man, due to techno-scientific and psycho-cosmic factors which will not be analyzed here, has lost the capacity, not to explain, but to understand his world and to interpret his relationship to it meaningfully. A failure of historical consciousness has bludgeoned man into a state of existential unconsciousness. The task for modern man, if he would regain a sense of resolute purposefulness and unequivocal directionability to his life, is to recover a consciousness of historicality *(Geschichtlichkeit)* of his own existence. Dilthey has convincingly suggested that life is experience in "individual moments of meaning," and that these moments of meaning "require the context of the past and the horizon of future expectations. . ." which can only be explained and understood in terms of the human dimension of historicality.[33] An understanding of the character and quality, origin and direction, of these "moments of meaning" is what our discussion of man as interpreter, interpretation as history, and history as meaning is all about. To illustrate how the concept of meaning can be employed as a *hermeneutical device* in grasping the meaning of our being is our last and pivotal point in this discussion, viz., meaning as hermeneutics.

The humanness of man is exemplified in his drive and ability to encounter and interpret a new dimension of reality beyond the physical environment, a world of symbols embodying an intrinsically historical discovery of meaning. Not only does human life illustrate the meaning of history, human life also embodies the history of meaning. "The dimension of meaning," explains Heschel, "is as indigenous to man's being human as the dimension of space is to stars and stones."[34] If our scenario is correct this far -- man as interpreter, interpretation as history, history as meaning -- then we are led resolutely to the crowning postulate of this development which is that meaning for man, whether created or discovered, is the interpretive mechanism par excellence by which he lives. **Meaning is hermeneutics.**

Technically speaking, "hermeneutics is the study of understanding," or more precisely, hermeneutics "is the study of the methodological principles of interpretation and explanation." Yet, though these definitions are correct in the academic sense of the word, they fail to reach at the heart of my intention. They fall short of the existentially human quality of my aphorism -- meaning as hermeneutics. Closer to the point is Ricouer's suggestion that "hermeneutics is the system by which the deeper significance is revealed beneath the manifest content."[36]

Our intention in developing this thought has led us to Heidegger's notion of the "hermeneutics of Dasein" outlined in the SEIN UND ZEIT (1927). Here, we see the temporality and existential roots of understanding which form the backdrop for man's interpretation of the meaningfulness of his being. Hermeneutics for Heidegger is the study of the understanding of the works of man, or more pointedly, an explanation of human existence itself. Interpretation as well as understanding are foundational modes of man's being. And the followers of Heidegger see hermeneutics as a philosophical exploration of the character and requisite conditions for all understanding and interpretation.[37]

Heidegger's contribution to hermeneutics is unquestionably significant, having marked a turning point in the development of both the term and the field. Hermeneutics has become at once linked both to the ontological and the existential dimensions of understanding and interpretation. Now, the definition of hermeneutics, thanks to Heidegger, deals with "the moment that meaning comes to light." In these moments, man interprets his world in terms of meaning, i.e., meaning as hermeneutics. And, these moments, as expressive of the historicality of man, are both cultural and religious in the sense that culture and religion are meaning-systems by means of which man grasps the new dimension of his own being in the world.

Meaning, as discussed earlier, carries with it the element of historicality, of temporality. Meaning does not exist merely in the abstract but profoundly manifests itself in the concrete, in the lived experience of the human community. Necessarily, then, if meaning is to function hermeneutically as the human mechanism for interpreting the world, meaning must function through those arenas of human experience most directly linked to encountering a world in need of interpretation. Those arenas are culture and religion.

The Princeton anthropologist, Clifford Geertz, has defined "man as a symbolizing, conceptualizing, meaning-seeking animal,"[38] who produces culture and religion as expressions of these characteristics. Culture, explains Geertz, is "an historically transmitted pattern of meanings embodied in symbols."[39] Accordingly, religion "is in part an attempt to conserve the fund of general meanings in terms of which each individual interprets his experience and organizes his conduct." In the same context, Geertz has suggested that man's compulsion to "make sense out of experience" is as characteristically human as man's biological needs. Thus, "to make sense out of experience" is what in the Heideggerian sense we are labelling hermeneutics, and it is by means of the meaning-systems of culture and religion that this "drive to interpret" most predictably, systematically, and fruitfully reveals itself.

We have been suggesting that meaning is the hermeneutical device or key by which man interprets his world in the sense that hermeneutics in the Heideggerian usage is "the analysis of human existence."[40] Whereas among the anthropologists, Geertz would propose that culture-analysis must focus upon the meaning-system embodied in cultural symbols, philosophers and theologians might likewise argue that religious-analysis must focus upon the meaning-system embodied in religious symbols. Heinrich Otto, a modern theologian, reportedly has said that "theology is really hermeneutics," whereas Carl Michaelson, another modern theologian, has suggested that systematic theology is "the hermeneutical analysis of being."

If Geertz is the modern anthropological exemplar of culture-analysis employing the concept of meaning as the interpretive key in his science, then Paul Tillich is unquestionably the modern theological exemplar of religious analysis employing the concept of meaning as the interpretive key in his discipline.[41] For Tillich, meaning is that from which all religious and cultural expressions receive their impetus. And he was, therefore, very impatient with any notion of a meaningless existence -- for him a notion impossible to entertain or defend. "Even the totality of meaning," Tillich once argued, "need not be meaningful, but rather could disappear, like every particular meaning in the abyss of meaninglessness, if the presupposition of an unconditional meaningfulness were not alive in every act of meaning."[42] For

Tillich, to raise the question or possibility of meaninglessness is to have already posited meaning.

Contrary to Sartre's existentialism,[43] Tillich insists that meaning is not a creation of man's own devices but rather a discovery which reveals the sustaining source of the human spirit. "Culture," reasons Tillich, "does not create this empty space of mere validity. It creates meaning as the actualization of what is potential in the bearer of the spirit -- in man."[44] Culture is not self-contained but rather points beyond its symbol-systems to that from which it derives its power for human creativity. Tillich argues that both culture and religion are meaning-systems, are mechanisms expressed through symbols by the human spirit, which converge in the creativity of man's quest to interpret his world. "Religion," he explains, "is directedness toward the Unconditional (the Unconditional meaning, toward the import of meaning), and culture is directedness toward the conditioned forms (of meaning) and their unity."[45] Having framed the relationship of culture and religion in terms of their shared convergence upon meaning as man's effort to grasp his world, Tillich has added another dimension to Geertz's approach to culture and religion analysis. Thus, Tillich establishes a symbiotic relationship between religion and culture in these terms: "In the cultural act, the religious is substantial; in the religious act, the cultural is formal."[46]

If culture is the experiential expression of meaning, or more correctly is the context within which and the socio-historical mechanism whereby meaning is both experienced and expressed, then the function of the concept of meaning is necessarily interpretational, or hermeneutical.[47] In closing, we might suggest that religion as an expression of meaning is a demonstration of mankind's quest to know and understand his world and his place in it. We might then, on the basis of the foregoing discussion, propose a set of definitions. Culture is that integrated complex of conceptual and empirical expressions of conditional and created meaning embodied within a socio-historical milieu. Religion is that integrated complex of conceptual and empirical expressions of unconditional and discovered meaning embodied within a socio-historical milieu.[48] By having defined religion and culture as meaning-systems, as arenas within which expressions of meaning converge, we have demonstrated the religio-cultural matrix of interpretation -- an interpretation of man's historicality wherein we can define religion and culture as meaning, and meaning as hermeneutics.

NOTES

1. Abraham Joshua Heschel, WHO IS MAN? (Stanford, Ca: Stanford University Press, 1968), p. 76.

2. Teilhard de Chardin, BUILDING THE EARTH (N.Y.: Avon Books, 1965), p. 105.

3. Martin Heidegger, KANT UND DAS PROBLEM DER METAPHYSIK (Frankfort: Klostermann, 1951).

4. As quoted in Martin Buber, BETWEEN MAN AND MAN (N.Y.: Macmillan: 1968), p. 182.

5. Rene Dubos, SO HUMAN AN ANIMAL (N.Y.: Charles Scribner's Sons, 1968), p. 14.

6. Ernst Cassirer, AN EASSY ON MAN   (New Haven: Yale University Press, 1969), p. 5.

7. Abraham Joshua Heschel, THE INSECURITY OF FREEDOM: ESSAYS ON HUMAN EXISTENCE (N.Y.: Schocken Books, 1972), p. 162.

8. Julian Marias, "Philosophic Truth and the Metaphoric System," in INTERPRETATION: THE POETRY OF MEANING, edited by Stanley Romaine Hopper and D. L. Miller (N.Y.: Harcourt, Brace & World, 1967), p. 48.

9. Cassirer, ESSAY ON MAN, p. 5.

10. For discussion see my "Ethnicity and the Future of Man: The Perspective of Teilhard de Chardin," THE TEILHARD REVIEW XI, 1 (Feb, 1976): 16-21.

11. Cassirer, ESSAY ON MAN, p. 24.

12. Paul Ricouer, "The Symbol Gives Rise to Thought," in LITERATURE AND RELIGION, edited by G. B. Gunn (N.Y.: Harper Forum, 1971), p. 213.

13. Susanne K. Langer, PHILOSOPHICAL SKETCHES (N.Y.: Mentor Books, 1964), p. 54.

14. Carl Gustav Jung, MODERN MAN IN SEARCH OF A SOUL (N.Y.: Harcourt, Brace, and World, 1933).

15. Peter L. Berger, the SACRED CANOPY: ELEMENTS OF A SOCIO-LOGICAL THEORY OF RELIGION (N.Y.: Anchor, 1969), p. 22.

16. Peter L. Berger, A RUMOR OF ANGELS: MODERN SOCIETY AND THE REDISCOVERY OF THE SACRED (N.Y.: Anchor, 1970), p. 53.

17. Wilhelm Dilthey, GESAMMELTE SCHRIFTEN, 14 volumes (Gottingen: Vandenhoeck and Ruprecht, 1913-1967), V:172.

18. Richard E. Palmer, HERMENEUTICS: INTERPRETATION THEORY IN SCHLEIERMACHER, DILTHEY, HEIDEGGER, AND GADAMER (Evanston, IL: Northwestern University Press, 1969), p. 118. Also see my "Religious Myth and Symbol: A Convergence of Philosophy and Anthropology," PHILOSOPHY TODAY, XVIII, 4 (Spring, 1974): 68-84.

19. As quoted in Cassirer, ESSAY ON MAN, p. 172.

20. Palmer, HERMENEUTICS, p. 242.

21. Cassirer, ESSAY ON MAN, pp. 174-175.

22. Dilthey, GESAMMELTE SCHRIFTEN, VII:140.

23. Palmer, HERMENEUTICS, p. 111.

24. Dilthey, GESAMMELTE SCHRIFTEN, VIII:224.

25. Otto Friedrich Bollnow, DIE LEBENSPHILOSOPHIE (Berlin: Springer, 1958).

26. Palmer, HERMENEUTICS, p. 117.

27. **Ibid.**, p. 120.

28. Cassirer, ESSAY ON MAN, p. 191.

29. Dilthey, GESAMMELTE SCHRIFTEN, VII:279.

30. Martin Heidegger, SEIN UND ZIET (Halle: Niemeyer, 1927), p. 37.

31. Dilthey as quoted by Palmer, HERMENEUTICS, p. 109.

32. Dilthey, GESAMMELTE SCHRIFTEN, VI:317.

33. dilthey as quoted by Palmer, HERMENEUTICS, p. 101.

34. Heschel, WHO IS MAN?, p. 51.

35. WEBSTER'S THIRD NEW INTERNATIONAL DICTIONARY.

36. Palmer, HERMENEUTICS, p. 44.

37. Heidegger's hermeneutics is carefully analyzed by Hans-Georg Gadamer, WAHRHEIT UND METHODE: GRUNZUGE EINER PHILOSOPHISCHEN HERMENEUTIK (Tubingen: J.C.B. Mohr, 1960).

38. Clifford Geertz, "Ethos, World-View and the Analysis of the Sacred Symbols," ANTIOCH REVIEW (Winter, 1957-58):436.

39. Clifford Geertz, "Religion as a Cultural System," in ANTHRO-POLOGICAL APPROACHES TO THE STUDY OF RELIGION, edited by M. Banton (Longon: Tavistock, 1966, p. 3.

40. Stanley Romaine Hopper, "The Poetry of Meaning," in LITERA-TURE AND RELIGION, p. 223.

41. For a critical comparison of Tillich and Geertz on this point, see Chapter Ten above, pp. 136 ff.

42. Paul Tillich, WHAT IS RELIGION? (N.Y.: Harper, 1969), p. 57.

43. For a critique of Sartre's use of the concept of "meaning," see my IN SEARCH OF MEANING: FROM FREUD TO TEILHARD DE CHARDIN (Washington, D.C.: University Press of America, 1978), pp. 15-23.

44. Paul Tillich, SYSTEMATIC THEOLOGY, 3 volumes (Chicago: University of Chicago Press, 1967), III:84.

45. Tillich, WHAT IS RELIGION?, p. 59.

46. **Ibid.**, p. 60.

47. See my "Clifford Geertz: An Interfacing of Anthropology and Religious Studies," HORIZONS, V, 2 (Winter, 1978):203-210.

48. This point is considered carefully in my "Theology and Symbol: An Anthropological Approach," JOURNAL OF RELIGIOUS THOUGHT, XXX, 3 (Fall, 1974):51-61.

John H. Morgan, an Episcopal priest, lives with his wife and three daughers on their family farm in Bristol, Indiana. He received the Doctor of Philosophy degree from the Hartford Seminary Foundation and the Doctor of Science degree from the London College of Applied Science. Dr. Morgan has served on the graduate behavioral science faculties of the University of Connecticut and the University of Texas.